CONVERSATIONS BEYOND THE LIGHT

COMMUNICATION WITH DEPARTED FRIENDS & COLLEAGUES BY ELECTRONIC MEANS

DR. PAT KUBIS and MARK MACY

Published by Griffin Publishing in conjunction with—

Continuing Life Research
Boulder, Colorado

CONVERSATIONS BEYOND THE LIGHT

Book design: Mark M. Dodge
Copy editor: Dina Falls
Photo editor: Robin Howland
Typesetting: Regina Books
Production supervision: Larry Davis

10 9 8 7 6 5 4 3 2 1

ISBN 1-882180-47-X

Published by Griffin Publishing in conjunction with—
Continuing Life Research
P.O. Box 11036
Boulder, CO 80301 USA

Manufactured in the United States of America

CONTENTS

Introduction

After first grasping the idea of death, young children often ask a variant of the question: "What happens after we die?" Parents are usually at a loss about how to answer, since they have not yet arrived at their own answer. Every culture, every generation, every individual wants to know the answer to: "If a man dies, shall he live again?" Even the space capsule sent by NASA out beyond our solar system contained questions asking possible other inhabitants of our universe if they had found an answer to the question of death.

The relevance of this question becomes apparent when we consider our life's purpose and the limited time we have to fulfill it. Does our consciousness come into existence only to be snuffed out at the end of our lifespan? Or are there levels or cycles of existence beyond the present "reality" which continue or carry further our earthly endeavors? If so, then every thought and action has meaning far beyond the present.

The advent of modern science led to the Enlightenment period of the 17th century and the belief that all problems could be solved by either reason or the scientific method. Galileo asked the Church fathers to look through his telescope and trust their five senses rather than to blindly believe church doctrine which held that earth is the center of our solar system. This empirical method of proof, i.e. posing a hypothesis and, with strict controls, guiding the experiment to its unbiased results, alas, led the Western mind to doubt all experiences not provable in this manner.

Yet always there were some who experienced events unexplainable by science or so-called rational thinking. The mystical union, the one-ness, experienced by Christian mystics, the Sufis of Islam, Native American Shamans, and described in the Jewish Kabala, cannot easily be dismissed. When Buddha admonished his followers to not unquestioningly accept his teachings, but to trust their experience, he was referring to not just the five senses, but also humans' inner, subjective experiences. These inner experiences of dimensions beyond our earthly life, while anecdotal, were until recently not verifiable by traditional methods. Our authors have taken on a task which clearly necessitates what physicist Thomas Kuhn calls the "new paradigm," i.e. to look at events from a whole new perspective, and in the authors' case explore the soul's transcendence beyond this earthly life of human consciousness.

The authors and the psychic laboratories they collaborated with, presented their findings with the help of sophisticated electronic equipment not available previously. Skeptics also object to reports of different kinds of so-called near-death-experience or NDE, first reported by Raymond Moody, M.D. While the majority of individuals declared clinically dead are transported through a tunnel toward a white light, others take a different, and some even extremely frightening journey. Likewise throughout the years, other realms of existence have been variously described by those who had them, as heaven or hell, nirvana or purgatory, bliss or the place of a thousand wrathful gods.

These disparate accounts added fuel to the fire of skeptics. However, the authors of *Conversations Beyond the Light* present a fresh point of view by describing the astral plane as multi-dimensional, consisting of seven levels. This helps us understand the varieties of near-death-experiences described in the literature over the last twenty years. It also gives us a better understanding of the many different descriptions and messages of those souls who are able to communicate with relatives and friends on this earthly plane.

Many volumes have been written about people able to contact spirit guides, are channelers, or give psychic readings. From the reports and experiences of the authors it appears that all of them could be true because of the much broader, multi-dimensional views given us by Mark Macy and Pat Kubis. In a foreword to W. Y. Evans-Wentz translation of *Tibetan Book of the Dead*, Lama Anagarika Govinda says:

> There is not *one* person, indeed, not *one* living being, that has *not* returned from death. In fact, we all have died many deaths, before we came into this incarnation. And what we call birth is merely the reverse side of death, like one of the two sides of a coin, or like a door which we call "entrance"

from outside and "exit" from inside a room....It is much more astonishing that not everyone remembers his or her previous death; and, because of this lack of remembering, most persons do not believe there was a previous death. But likewise, they do not remember their recent birth and yet they do not doubt that they were recently born.

While until the recent past only the rare visionary delved into the realms our authors refer to as "beyond the light," interest in these transpersonal dimensions now comes from many quarters. And best of all, Macy and Kubis offer their readers a concrete method by which they can explore for themselves realms that proved until now too difficult to explore.

Elton Davis, Ed.D.
Professor Emeritus
Pasadena City College

Prologue

In 1976, the great yogi Sant Keshavadas casually remarked at a lecture in India that by the end of the century, we would be able to pick up a phone and "call" friends, loved ones, and colleagues who have died.

Even before that, in 1936, theosophist Alice Bailey predicted that those who had passed over will communicate with Earth and this communication will be "reduced to a true science.... Death will lose its terrors, and that particular fear will come to an end."[1] Today, in Luxembourg, and in many countries all over the world, the prophecies of Bailey and Sant Keshavadas have come true.

A new science is being born, the science of Instrumental Transcommunication (ITC). Today, using high-tech communication, the "dead" are now *transmitting* information to our scientists in pictures, text, and voice via television screens, computers and telephones. Now, a "deceased" scientist can speak via television to a roomful of scientists on earth. The undisputed leaders of this new science of ITC, Jules and Maggy Harsch-Fischbach, who run the Transcommunication Study Circle of Luxembourg (CETL), received the Swiss Award for Paranormal

[1]*Handbook of PSI Discoveries* by Sheila Ostrander & Lynn Schroeder, Berkeley Publishing Corp., p.264.

Discoveries in Bern in 1992. Right now, in Luxembourg, Germany, and other countries, various TV programs are tracing the development of ITC.

Dozens of "dead scientists," including Thomas Alva Edison, Albert Einstein, Madame Curie, and their colleagues, are engaged in a project to communicate with the Earth. *This is not science fiction.* It is happening daily in sound labs in the United States, Australia, Austria, Belgium, England, Germany, France, Luxembourg, Italy, the Netherlands, Spain, Sweden and Switzerland.

Curiously, the Bible says (1 Cor. 15:26) "The last enemy to be destroyed is death." While many theologians have noted the enigmatic scripture, it is doubtful any of them could even imagine how the grim reaper was to be destroyed. Yet, today, in our time, the dead are transmitting their faces on television, transmitting the locale where they live, and describing their lives in their afterlife locale. All of the evidence documented by scientists and research groups on Earth indicates that there is no death, that individuality continues in another dimension.

In Luxembourg, a distraught mother can "hook up" via television with her deceased son, who sends a picture of himself smiling and very much alive in another dimension. A grief-stricken family can communicate with a young son who was brutally murdered and see that he is happy and healed of his wounds.

We are privileged to be living in this most astounding time, when some of the greatest mysteries of life—its purpose and design—are being revealed. Some of the world's churches will find their teachings vindicated; others will have to meet the challenge of new scientific data. Amazingly, the Vatican has known of the research on Instrumental Transcommunication for years and even has authorized its own research people to explore the subject.[1] Reincarnation, which has been regarded as only a philosophic doctrine, is now corroborated by the dead who are quite alive in another dimension.

How this greatest of all discoveries began is a story as compelling as the discovery of atomic science. Even more compelling is the array of over 1000 spirit scientists and colleagues in a world beyond our own, who are committing their existence and their talents to this vast project. At last, the "veil of death" has been penetrated!

---

[1]*Handbook of Psi Discoveries*, p. 267.

1

The World of the Dead

DEATH IS A NEW BEGINNING

Ernst Mackes died on November 26, 1992. He was a good friend of Maggy and Jules Harsch-Fischbach, Directors of CETL,[1] a paranormal lab in Luxembourg investigating the continuity of life after death. When Maggy turned on her computer, on February 4, 1993, she found a message from Ernst. "Jules," she cried to her husband, "it's from Ernst." Excited, they watched the printer print out a text from another dimension.

> At the moment I am sitting here under a roof of exotic palm tree leaves. I am trying to focus my thoughts into a sort of typewriter which is sitting in front of me on the glass plate of a small bamboo table.... As you know, on Nov. 26 (1992) the body of Ernst Mackes was definitely left in the Earthly dimension and my spiritual power [my soul] was

[1]Cercle D'Etudes sur la Transcommunication, Luxembourg.

set free. During the last few years, it could magnify only weakly over my sick body.

...I was in the position of a pilot who could not control his aircraft anymore. But all this is over and now I am here on Marduk and have finally found my beloved Margret [his deceased wife] again. When I arrived here I was understandably confused. Because of my illness, I could not immediately think or see clearly.

With the help of friendly people, among them my father and other former acquaintances from Earth, I soon learned to use my mental and physical powers effectively again.

...Wounds and amputations take some time to heal and regenerate here. Old age reverts backwards. Every hour, one slowly feels a strength flow back into the body that was lost long ago. For people who are mentally disabled, this recovery happens slowly and in steps.

I am now the old Ernst again...or should I say the new Ernst! Above me is the light of our three suns. Temperatures are very moderate, and in the clear morning air numerous multicolored hummingbirds are buzzing around me. Butterflies of incredible beauty, some of them as large as soup plates, are flapping their wings and settle down on blossoms and plants.

Before me is a refreshing glass of lemonade. In the distance the sunlight is reflecting in the River of Eternity which is visible behind a yellow sand beach. Margret and I often swim in the pleasant water and enjoy our newly discovered young bodies.

On March 4, 1993, CETL received a scanned picture of the now much younger Ernst on their computer. Spirit technicians at Timestream Space Lab, a superhigh-technology communications lab located in the spirit world, planted the scanned image on the computer's hard disk. (See Plate 1)

This was all in a day's work for Maggy and Jules at CETL, who for the past six years have been receiving messages from the dead via television, telephone, radio, tape recorder and computer.

The account of life after death provided by Ernst Mackes tallies with the experiences of other deceased researchers who, after death, find themselves alive on the astral plane.[1]

In their communications with CETL, their experiences are remarkably similar:

> We have a body like yours. It consists of finer matter and vibration than your dense, coarse physical bodies. There is no sickness here. Missing limbs regenerate. Bodies that are disfigured on Earth become perfect. We live in comfortably furnished houses. The countryside is very beautiful. The average age of people here is 25-30 years. Persons who die of old age on Earth wake up here after a regenerating sleep.
>
> This sleep lasts approximately 6 weeks of Earth time. With some persons it may be less.

Spirit communicators say people have their original hair, teeth and other body parts and, yes, sex does indeed exist there; but without pregnancy.

Communicators add that those people who have had a debilitating illness or who have been mutilated by accident or murder, need a brief recuperative period to restore the astral body to its healthy, normal state.

---

[1] An invisible plane or world composed of finer atoms, which shares the same space as earth. Many religions say it is where the spirit temporarily resides after death—"the Spirit World."

Thoughts of disease or mutilation are carried in the mind and are mind constructs or templates. Disease depletes the energy body. It takes time for the energy body to regenerate and for the healing technicians to help reveal to the newly dead person that he or she is no longer sick or maimed. For example, the person with an amputated leg carries a strong mind construct or template of a missing leg. Even though the astral body is perfect, how the person "sees" the self in his or her mind has a great deal to do with how the astral body appears to others. When the healing technicians are able to convince the person that his or her visualization of self controls the appearance of the astral body, then the person is able to create the desired image of self.

Consequently, most people on the astral plane choose to depict themselves at an age when they were healthiest and most handsome or beautiful—their prime. Yet if wearing glasses is part of that image of self, the person may choose to depict himself or herself with glasses. Yogis say that masters who travel the astral plane often choose an older astral body simply for the benefit of their disciples who are used to seeing their master in an older body. The main point is that the astral plane is a world of energy and thoughts control energy.

The information about the astral plane that Jules and Maggy Harsch-Fischbach are slowly but surely gathering at last provides hard evidence of what the kingdom of the dead is like—but the data paints, instead, a picture of a "kingdom" of the very much alive. Perhaps Plato was right. He insisted that we are the ones who are dead and that the dead are really alive.

One former colleague, Friedrich Juergenson, who died in 1987 and joined the staff of Timestream on the astral plane, reported in 1993:

> All thoughts are basically nothing but telepathy. In our view the human eye is blind, for it prevents the recognition of existing possibilities and extra-sensory perception. A blind person in your reality is better off in the spiritual sense than a person with eyesight.

Scientists on the other side say that communication on the astral plane is telepathic so they do not need larynxes or other speech equipment which is necessary to human beings. However, their lack of speech organs has made communication with those who live on Earth difficult. Until now. With the advent of television, computers, and fax machines, those on the astral plane have been able to build an electronic bridge which makes communication between the two worlds possible. The research that employs such electronic bridges to contact the spirit worlds is called Instrumental Transcommunication or ITC.

Experimenters in ITC receive images, text and simulated voices from their spirit colleagues, who say they can "manufacture" voices reminiscent of their Earth voices by the use of apparatuses on their side of the veil. These apparatuses can "soak up" noise on Earth (such as the hiss between radio stations) and turn it into artificial voices.

ITC of this type is fairly new, having begun in the mid-1980s. Before that, in the 1950s, "the dead" began to make contact through audiotapes. Research was conducted by thousands of people—much of it under strict laboratory conditions—and hundreds of thousands of short, faint spirit voices were collected over the years. One man, a Latvian psychologist named Konstantin Raudive, collected over seventy-five thousand voices on tapes and documented over fifteen thousand of them. He presented his research in a book, *Breakthrough*, which startled the scientific community. Raudive, using an ordinary tape recorder, would sit quietly alone, address departed friends and loved ones, and ask them questions. Then he would let the tape recorder run in his laboratory for several hours, monitoring it. The dead answered his questions and explained that they could modulate sound waves with their thoughts to simulate voice patterns. They told him to turn a radio on in the laboratory and to tune it between stations, where static or "white noise" was present. They then used the vibrations of the white noise to create words. They also said they had developed an apparatus which helped them to make the voice patterns audible.

Today CETL, and a growing number of other sound labs throughout the world, are engaged in ITC experiments with the spirit group Timestream, who says its facilities are located in the third plane of the astral world on a planet named Marduk.

Spirit workers describe Timestream, whose purpose is to communicate with Earth, as being the size of a large cathedral with very advanced video and sound equipment, so advanced that it has been having a hard time communicating with us because our equipment is so primitive.

The Director of Timestream is a scientist, Swejen Salter, who reports that she was born, lived and died on the planet Varid, a parallel planet of Earth. Since her death in 1987 (approximate Earth time) she has been living on the astral planet, Marduk. She leads a small team of experimenters—among them Thomas Alva Edison, Marie Curie, Wernher von Braun, and Albert Einstein—all who are part of the large group of colleagues in the spirit group Timestream. The Timestream group is in daily contact with colleagues in sound labs in various countries. At present, those countries include the United States, Australia, Austria, Belgium, Brazil, China, England, France, Germany, Italy, Japan, Luxembourg, the Netherlands and Sweden.

The Timestream research team also includes Konstantin Raudive (now deceased, but very much alive on the astral plane), as well as Friedrich Juergenson and Klaus Schreiber, both of whom when living on Earth were key researchers in spirit audio and video transmissions. Other members of the team are Dr. Konrad Lorenz, father of modern ethology; writers Sir Conan Doyle and Jules Verne; and explorer Sir Richard Francis Burton. Filmmakers George Cukor and Hal Roach provide film expertise to help with artistic considerations in television transmission. A key point these researchers are establishing is that one can continue one's work, if one wishes, on the other side. (See Plates 9-12)

On October 4th, 1986, CETL received its first video image from their spirit partners. Maggy and Jules recorded it on a VHS recorder with a Panasonic A-2 video camera. The image of a man, Pierre K, appeared on the TV screen for a duration of 4/50ths of a second. Earlier they had received audio transmissions from Pierre via a previously established "electronic bridge" known as the "Euro Signal Bridge," and had recorded them on tape. But now they could actually see him! Being CETL's first paranormal video image, the picture of Pierre K was quite hazy and distorted. Still, Pierre K's family identified him immediately.

Soon CETL began receiving many paranormal video images from the spirit world, including one of a former friend and colleague, Hanna Buschbeck. Hanna had been working with audio transmission, but had recently passed away. She had been living in Heilbronn, Germany and founded the German Electronic Voice Association to track and document early paranormal sound research in Europe.

The first video transmissions only lasted a split second. The major technical difficulty preventing longer transmissions was the primitive audio and visual equipment in use on Earth. Spiritside colleagues began making suggestions about how to improve the equipment. However, a major technical problem was encountered when it was found that certain metals existing in their subtle dimension do not exist in our dense physical world. Substitutions had to be made, and finding the right substitute took time.

As new equipment was developed and modified, longer picture sequences came through as well as pages and pages of computer text.

Through practical experience, however, CETL soon learned that the biggest obstacle to ITC contacts is not technical in nature. It involves the "energy field" that is created when two or more beings become aware of each other. This field is then strengthened when the beings start collaborating in a close psychic and spiritual rapport. CETL scientists call this a "contact field," and it doesn't matter how advanced the equipment or the level of expertise, real success cannot be achieved in ITC contacts until this contact field is firmly established across dimensions.

Spirit scientists warn that the reception of their messages can be seriously affected by mankind's thoughts, which are nothing more than energy vibrations:

> Aggressive, fearful attitudes prevent the further development of good, noise-free, two-way voice communication with other dimensions, and it is time that this is said. Some people would be shocked to know how destructive their thoughts can be to themselves and to the bridge-building efforts of the other side. Transcommunication is like a sensitive net of vibrations which can only spread out in the world if people can find mutual understanding. We each should strive for a level of progression where we no longer need to attack our fellow man.

So even though communication can occur through television and phone, the CLARITY of transmission depends on the contact field, the thoughts of those receiving the transmission. Maggy and Jules discovered, at their large open meetings, that if a group of people had negative thoughts about ITC, their negative vibrations seriously affected the vibrations coming from the astral plane.

However, Timestream scientists believe that as more and more powerful equipment is developed, the contact field will not be nearly as important as it is now. Using the progression of television as an analogy, it could be explained like this: when television was first introduced, signals were weak, and if there were any mountains or trees in the way the reception was extremely poor. Now, with the use of satellites and cable, a good, strong television signal can be received virtually anywhere regardless of the previous obstacles.

By 1993, television transmission was beginning to play a less important role in the overall ITC project. The research team on the other side was now able to access the hard drives of computers on Earth and to leave detailed, computer-scanned images as well as several pages of text. The computer-scanned images were far more detailed and less subject to distortion than the video images.

Researchers on Earth can direct questions to researchers on the other side and receive answers by telephone, radio, TV, computer or, in late 1993, even by fax. Recently, phone calls from Konstantin Raudive of Timestream were received in Luxembourg, Germany, the U.S., Brazil, Sweden, China and Japan, over three month period.

CETL in Luxembourg receives an average of three paranormal telephone calls per week.

WHAT'S BEHIND THESE TRANSMISSIONS FROM THE SPIRIT WORLD?

When Maggy and Jules were just starting out in the summer of 1986, a high-pitched, mechanical sounding voice was received on an FM tuner and the entity identified himself as a higher being who had no name. "Call me Technician," he said. He gave Maggy and Jules instructions on how to modify the equipment at the Luxembourg lab for better reception. He had the memory of a computer and said he had never lived on Earth. But he was an important part of the research team on the other side. He went on to say:

I am not human, I never incarnated, I am not and never was an animal. I am not energy and I am not a light being. You are familiar with the picture of two children walking across the bridge under the protection of a higher being [an angel]. This is what I am to you, but without the wings. You can call me Technician. I am assigned to the planet Earth.

Some of the researchers at CETL regard him as an angelic being and some as a doorkeeper between two dimensions. Recently, the Technician told of the difficulties the spirit workers have had in building a mediumistic bridge, or contact field, to us on Earth. This endeavor has been going on for many years, he explained. The process of building the bridge has involved a growing relationship of love, trust and unity of thought between the workers on Earth and in the spirit world. The Technician said:

You are living in a time when truth is easily distorted and false speculations about eternal life are quickly passed out as the only truth. God prefers the seeker and those who question. No efforts are spared to advance human thinking and individual initiative from its low animal instincts to a position of spiritual thinking.

The Technician plainly indicated that while the communication project directed from the other side was scientific in nature, it was also spiritual and that he was the philosophic mentor of the spirit research team. As ITC advances, Earth is gaining ever easier access to current descriptions of the afterworld, complete with hard evidence, to supplement the rich religious descriptions of human heritage.

At last our scientists could ask, "What kind of life can man expect on the other side?"—and have a good chance for a realistic reply. What we have learned so far is that the physical universe is but a small part of creation, that all worlds throughout this immense universe are composed of pure consciousness, and that the number one law of life everywhere is:

Thoughts Create Reality.

We have received pages of computer text describing lush landscapes with beautiful, fragrant flowers, ponds, lakes, mountains, butterflies, birds, animals, and even deceased family pets waiting for their owners. Television pictures beamed to Earth show the landscapes and people interacting in those landscapes.

Researchers on the other side tell us that children who die on Earth arrive on the mid-astral plane or the third plane and are either cared for by relatives who have died before them or they are cared for by people who love children [see Chapter Five for description of spirit planes]. The children grow and develop until they have reached the average age of twenty-five to thirty years.

On the astral plane, animals, too, are cared for by either their owners who have died or people who love animals. Just as the physical universe is rich with planets (many of which are no doubt inhabited by physical life), there are many "astral" planets comprising what is called the astral plane or astral dimension, where most people on Earth awaken after they die.

Richard Francis Burton, writer and world traveler, and part of Timestream's team, has been busy since his death in 1890. He is charting the world where Timestream is located, and says that a large river, the River of Eternity, runs through the entire planet, "like a snake biting its own tail."

Clustered along the river are communities of people bonded together by ideas of culture, religion, and race. American Indians, who once lived on the great plains, still live in teepees. Here are the Happy Hunting Grounds of which the Indians speak.

Communities of Catholics, Muslims, Hindus, Christians, Jews, Christian Scientists, all live according to the faith they espoused. On this plane, the old proverb holds true: "Birds of a feather flock together." In a sense, heaven is what you believe it is. And that is the point. "Heaven" is a dream world. It's what you believe it is. However, it is as real to all the people who live there as our world is to us.

There is also growth in the astral world. Once a person is able to break through the idea boundaries, a new type of existence is possible.

The astral plane is vast. Swejen Salter says that approximately sixty billion humanoids gather here from all existing worlds. Our spirit friends tell us:

> We eat and drink like you do. Our nourishment is "synthetic," i.e. we materialize Earthly food, so to speak. The meat, which some people still like, is only a reproduction of real matter. No animal has to die for another living being.

Still, one's personality and character do not change by dying. Nor does one become all knowing. To assume that our spirit colleagues at Timestream have all the answers would be a mistake. They can only report the environment where they live. They have not seen "God" from the third plane, but they do know that there are higher planes and that it is possible for the more spiritually advanced to visit or move to those planes.

Our spirit friends do acknowledge what all world religions have said through the ages: the totality of existence is understood only by the Cosmic Source, or God, or Atman, or Brahman.

Dying does not make you omniscient. There are yet higher mysteries to understand. Also, if you believe that dying will save you from your emotional problems, you'll probably find the problem still there. It seems that Earth is the best place to work out problems and situations.

On the astral plane, you create your reality, but it is a dream world. You may theorize many things and mentally change things instantly. On the astral plane, if you try to murder someone, you would find that you couldn't, no matter how hard you tried, since the spirit does not die. However, on Earth, if you murder someone, that person would be physically dead and you would have to face the consequences of your act. A life and its destiny pattern would be disrupted as would the lives of the victim's friends and loved ones. In other words, Earth teaches you hard lessons and it is literally the school of hard knocks. It confronts you with your actions and the consequences of your actions. It tests you as to what you really believe in.

The length of time people live on the astral plane spans a few weeks to hundreds of years. Then, if there is more to learn, they reincarnate (accept another body) on Earth, or perhaps on another inhabited planet. If they have learned everything they needed to learn, they will move up into a higher plane, or higher state of consciousness; for that is what the planes really are: states of consciousness.

Project director Swejen Salter describes the third plane's environment:

The River of Eternity stretches out approximately 100 million kilometers. Along its banks live those who were once living on Earth. ...Vegetation varies from algae to mammoth trees. Many buildings are made of wood. Some people or animals wake up here born anew. ...Others...come to us as old people and turn young again after the regenerating sleep. Why there are such differences, we do not know. ...Animals will be of an age of vitality and well being. ...Damaged tissue or broken bones regenerate just like a wound healing in your world, perfectly. Lost limbs will regrow. The blind will see again. ...The color of your hair and skin cannot be changed and will be the same as it was during your Earth life. Here in the river world, beings arrive from all levels of life.

Swejen Salter and her "life" companion, Sir Richard Francis Burton, speak of taking exploratory trips along the river in Burton's ship, Thrakka, and seeing snowy white polar caps, fog along the river, blue skies, and tree-covered hills at the foot of high mountains.

In the land of the dead are skyscrapers, and homes that range from thatch-roofed houses to magnificent palaces with glass towers and roofs of gold. Any kind of housing the mind can conceive is here; for in this world of energy these are mental creations: the dream houses we dream of owning.

Swejen Salter says she was thirty-eight when she died in an accident. Death came suddenly and she was not prepared. She awoke on a recliner in a cheerfully decorated room that she'd never seen before. She was greeted by Sir Richard Francis Burton, who was to become her close companion. Later, she joined him in his exploration of the astral plane. She felt very happy in this new dimension, but it was still not easy to adapt to a new life when she was torn away from a life of responsibilities on her home planet.

Her planet, Varid, was more advanced than Earth in its knowledge of life after death, and while she knew about the continuation of life, it was still an intellectual concept. She compared her death and rebirth to moving to a foreign country which is very nice but adjustments to the new living conditions must be made.

She discovered that on the third plane of the astral world, it is more difficult to avoid spiritual laws. As she says: "If you harbor bad intentions and thoughts, you will not be here very long." She explained that negative thoughts and attitudes immediately attract you to lower planes where people are still acting out their private dramas of lust, greed and selfishness. In this world, you can't ignore feelings and inclinations, nor can you suppress your wishes. If you have certain deeply felt Earthly desires, you will have to return to Earth to fulfill them.

Deceased researcher, Konstantin Raudive, remarks that he found his true self on the third level of consciousness. On Earth he had tried to be something else than he was, as do most people on Earth. "Today," he said happily, "in this world, I can acknowledge my own true self."

In essence, the astral plane is not the ultimate end of being. It is an interim place. Here, people can experience a heavenly refuge, patterned after what they have believed heaven would be like. They live here for a time and then either move up into a higher plane of consciousness or they return to Earth to learn new lessons, new concepts, to try out a life of which they've only dreamed. Some of the spirit research colleagues have already reincarnated back to Earth to continue working on the Transcommunication project from this side.

Not everyone qualifies for life on the astral plane when they die. Those who rejected the idea of life after death or never thought much about it may find themselves reincarnating very quickly. Also, if they suppressed their feelings, desires and talents, and led a material life that only served material aims, they will probably find themselves back on Earth again.

For example, a man who only thinks of making money or playing golf finds little satisfaction on the astral plane. As this is a "plane of dreams" where people create their own realities, they are the "star actors" in their self created script. While this sounds "heavenly," it can get boring after awhile.

The trouble is that if money is one's aim, one is immediately surrounded by it and there is no competition in getting it. Think of it and it's there. Nor is there any competition for the golfer. He or she can have a hole in one every day, and play a perfect game every time.

On the other hand, artists, philosophers, musicians, and scientists appreciate the chance to create their inventions in a peaceful world without the burdensome necessity of having to make a living and support a family. Consequently, they may choose to live on the astral plane for some time.

The astral plane is a plane of consciousness. Many people will find a temporary reward for their lives, but it is not permanent. There are higher worlds, higher dimensions—and above all, there is the world of the Creator. To reach that exalted plane takes the most committed of souls and Swejen Salter says that those who reach that highest of planes are never seen again.

2

Two Children on the Third Plane—

A BOY WHO LOVED FIREWORKS—AND JUERGEN WHO WAS MURDERED

It was every parent's worst nightmare come true. The Brauns' eight-year-old boy, Ezra, had been sick— a cold and fever that turned out to be much more serious. When all the tests were over, the doctors called the Brauns in. "Your boy has leukemia," they said. Then came the shock, the tears of denial, the stubborn refusal to accept the worst, the prayers and the fierce struggle to help Ezra overcome the wasting disease overtaking his body. The Brauns did everything within their power to save him. They had been missionaries. They called upon God to save their son. After all, hadn't they given their lives for God?

But the boy grew weaker and increasingly pale. He managed to live another four years and four months. Then early one morning, he crawled into their bed and cried heartbreakingly. He knew he was going to die. They all knew it. The Brauns held him tightly, as if by holding him, they could keep his precious spirit pulsating in his beating heart, as if they could keep him alive by will alone. The boy had grown old and wise in his illness. He looked like a weary, little old man. He was ready to go, he told his parents who knew now that no matter what they did it was time to say good-bye.

But what was there to say?

As the boy's father clasped him, he remembered how often Ezra had persuaded his parents to watch all the TV shows broadcast from Germany and Luxembourg on Instrumental Transcommunication. Abruptly, Ezra blurted that he would try to contact them on recording tapes later on. His father nodded and Ezra stopped crying. He died nine days later, on September 20, 1986. He was twelve years old.

His mother now keeps a poem that Ezra had written when he was eight years old:

> If I could only plug in a magic hat, I could become an astronaut.
> I would fly to the moon to look at everything,
> Then I would walk to the stars and to the sun.
> I would love to walk across the sky and sleep on clouds.

In December 1986, Ezra's parents were experimenting with a tape recorder when they heard an unknown voice on the tape, saying: "Ezra is waiting." A little later, another voice said, "I have LONG hair!" To the Brauns, this was a very evidential contact, for Ezra had been undergoing chemotherapy and had lost all his hair four times. They reported the contact to Maggy at CETL, who recorded the message in her journal. By this time CETL had already collected thousands of voices on tapes. Bits and pieces of people's lives—and afterlives. Some of them would fit into a solved puzzle and others would just remain scraps of unused information.

Some time later, Maggy received a letter from Salter:

> I know Ezra! He joined a Chinese group. He is sending greetings to his parents. He asks you to tell them that he has a head full of beautiful hair again. He has a penchant for fireworks.
>
> The Chinese people here organize occasional beautiful fireworks which anyone can watch. Ezra plays an important part in it. He would like his parents to know that he is not the boy who died of cancer anymore. He has grown into a fine young man who is now in his twenties.

Maggy contacted Ezra's parents and she received a letter back from Ezra's parents recounting the events leading up to his death in 1986 and his chemotherapy. Now, the tape with Ezra's remarks about having a full head of hair was an important piece of a puzzle that was beginning to come together.

In September 1990, Maggy received more information about Ezra. Salter said, "Ezra loves fireworks and takes an active part in it. We recently were observing such fireworks together."

Then, right before New Year's day, December 31, 1992, Maggy was getting ready for a small New Year's celebration party at home. The phone rang. It was Salter. She said she was working on a computerized picture transmission which she planned to send to CETL. "If everything goes well," she said, "you will find two pictures combined into one. One picture shows Ezra Braun, the other one is for yourself and is something to cheer you up." (See Plates 16 & 17)

Curious, Maggy started the scanning program. The pictures had already been stored as a file in the computer. Accessing the file, she saw a picture of a happy, dark-haired boy, shown from the waist up, standing in front of a tree in bloom, smiling, his arm raised. Over his shoulder was a heavy strap with a buckle.

Maggy thought wistfully that the blooming tree in the spirit world looked so beautiful, considering the cold, bleak weather in Luxembourg.

Also in that file was a picture of Maggy's own horse, who had died. She almost wept, realizing Salter had sent the picture of her horse, alive on the other side, as a gift for her. She also knew Salter had sent it to her so that people would know that our animal friends also continue life in spirit.

A few minutes later, Salter checked in again by phone:

> Tell me if everything arrived well. Unfortunately, I can't check from here if our experiment succeeded. It took a lot of work to send those pictures.

Maggy confirmed that the picture transmission had succeeded and she said, "I see that Ezra wears a strap across one shoulder. Also you picked a beautiful tree as a background."

Salter replied,

> The strap belongs to the bag that he always carries around with him. Remember, I once told you that he is very interested in the work of Paracelsus[1] who

---

[1]Swejen refers to Paracelsus (1490-1541), a physician and alchemist, who is very interested in teaching his healing methods to young people and older physicians, too. He is still living on the astral plane and Swejen says he is learning to use the computer.

is teaching Ezra about natural healing with plants and herbs. As far as I know Ezra collects these and saves them in his bag. Paracelsus is thrilled by the variety of herbs he finds. His zeal of collecting is infectious. He inspires the young people. He hopes to work out methods of healing which he can pass along to you. The tree is a cherry tree in full bloom.

Salter chuckled, continuing, "Ezra is Paracelsus' assistant, but whenever he really needs him, the boy's hard to find. The young people tease Paracelsus as much as he teases them. There is a lot of horseplay that goes on.... When you pass on the news to Ezra's parents, give them my greetings." (See Plate 18)

She added, "You will hear from me again, soon." Then she wished Maggy a Happy New Year and said, "Although the New Year's celebration has lost its meaning for us, many people here still celebrate it along with you in memory of their life on Earth." Similarly, other messages from Timestream have indicated that like New Year's, people in spirit enjoy celebrating birthdays and other special occasions with their families on Earth.

Maggy closed the contact with Salter, genuinely grateful for her friend in another dimension.

When the clock struck twelve and Maggy's neighbors were celebrating, she abruptly thought of Ezra and the others at Timestream sharing the celebration in their invisible dimension. She smiled, printing out a copy of the scanned picture of Ezra in the computer and sent it to the Brauns along with Salter's message.

Maggy received back an excited letter from the Brauns that further added to the mosaic of the boy Ezra. Ezra's parents said that even though Ezra had grown, they still recognized his infectious smile and there was no doubt the picture was of their son. His father filled in more information about the mosaic of Ezra Braun:

> You did not know our connections to China. I was required to stay in Beijing for two and a half months and was allowed to take my family with me for three weeks (in spite of medical warning for Ezra). We took him along because of his persistent begging. He always dreamed of taking a walk on the Great Wall of China.... When my wife and the children had to fly back on August 21, he cried and said: "I would like to stay in China forever! ...We were amused by your mention of fireworks. Nothing gave Ezra as much pleasure as setting off firecrackers. Only six weeks before his death he arranged [with the help of his friends] a wild and noisy display on the roof terrace and the burning of little paper boats on the water surface....

Then he added a note about the strap on Ezra's shoulder:

> This strap is part of a shoulder bag used by Chinese students until the middle of the 80's and beyond. During his visit in Beijing, Ezra saw such a shoulderbag carried by his Chinese companion. Upon return he wanted one himself. His wish was fulfilled. The bag accompanied him until his death and served as a container for all his little treasures and secrets. We still have the bag and it still contains almost everything he carried around during the last part of his life.

In July of 1993, Maggy received more information about Ezra. Salter sent a report that he was now studying medicine within the medical group of Timestream:

> He has established a special connection to the Chinese physician Yang Fudse who joined us only a short time ago. Ezra has learned much from this

physician. Yang Fudse has an excellent understanding of body, mind, and matter.

Further information came through on the computer
about Yang Fudse, *written in Chinese characters, by
Yang Fudse himself, even though the computer didn't have
a program to use Chinese characters.* The Chinese
physician claimed to have lived under the rule of
Shun Ti in the capital of Yo Lang in the years 150 to
200 AD.

Maggy explained, "Our PC, although capable of
almost 50 types of writing, cannot type out Chinese
letters."

With the help of a code sent to the lab for research
purposes, Maggy was able to transfer an answer to
Yang-Fudse from their computer's western alphabet
into Chinese. She didn't know if the Chinese symbols
would give the same meaning as a correct Chinese
letter written by a Chinese language expert. However,
the spiritside mentor, the Technician, assured Maggy
that Yang-Fudse would understand the writing—
though it would not be good enough for an expert.

Ezra's story reveals a life of growth and learning on
the third plane. He died as a boy and now on the
third plane is a young man learning Chinese
medicine. He is living with a group of Chinese
people, in a culture he very much admired. He is
happy and his earth experience now seems only a
dream. Again, the point Timestream stresses is that
we are all eternal creatures and each incarnation
experience we have is only an infinitesimal part of
our eternal life.

Ezra's parents feel specially blessed to have had this
transcommunication experience with their son. The
parents wrote to Maggy:

We are aware that few people can be given such a present. We feel obliged to let those in similar situations know about it. Perhaps they can handle the loss of their loved ones better and learn to live with it.

However, to Ezra's parents, the experience was a heart-break. They still felt the grief and loss of their son; but, on the other hand, they knew he was alive and even happy. It, of course, is hard to accept that they were only part of his Earth dream and a very short dream at that. But they know, too, that they will see Ezra again. And it will be a very happy reunion!

Maggy was soon to be involved in another communication between a mother and her child. During an ITC conference in Erzhausen, Germany, on May 26, 1991, a woman handed Maggy a letter but asked her not to open it until the end of the conference. When Maggy returned home, she remembered the letter and opened it. The letter was signed by a group of women ITC experimenters who asked her to contact Swejen Salter in the hopes that Salter would search for a small boy on the third plane who had been brutally murdered. The boy's name was Juergen Marcel. His mother couldn't stop grieving and they felt it would help her if she could achieve some kind of contact with her boy.

Maggy, a schoolteacher, and her husband Jules, a civil servant, both had to return to work the next day. Maggy, feeling the mother's pain, planned to write a long letter on her Commodore C64 computer to Salter. Before she had time to write that letter, a message about little Juergen came through on the computer from no less an illustrious person than Thomas of Canterbury whose life dates had been 1120-1170. The message had come from Station

Central, another spirit sound lab on the third plane. Spirits are telepathic; they can read one's thoughts, particularly if there is a strong emotional field connected to the thought.

The message came through on Maggy's computer, addressed to Juergen's mother in middle English. Translated, it read:

> Mother Liselgunde, you saw your child killed and yet your little Juergen Marcel lives now, I assure you. There is no doubt. Certainly, a horrible murder. There is no use denying it. Now weep no more. Take comfort with right good cheer. There is a better life in another place. This instrument, this MEZA, although it has mistakes, still we have good hope to build it and then we shall test it. Believe this as strongly as you have faith. And to researchers, I advise you to be in harmony [accord] with your opponents and to have peace with them. The dissent begins by another man and, whereas the reconciliation begins by yourself, I do not say that you shall run after your opponents for the sake of peace but that they shall be driven to it. Now friends of CETL, eat your meal and I wish you all the best I can think of.
>
> Thomas

A few days after receiving the message from Thomas, Maggy spoke with Salter about Juergen Marcel.

Salter described the boy as a friendly little boy with curly blonde hair and said: "The poor child had suffered many knife wounds on his head before he arrived here."

Maggy had forgotten that new arrivals still carry their wounds when they get there. "Who takes care of Juergen Marcel?" she asked curiously. "What happens to the wounded?"

"Juergen," Salter answered, "is in the care of Marie Mreches [a grandmother].... She treats his wounds and takes good care of him, as if he were her own child. The boy has forgotten what happened to him and plays happily with other children."

"But how was he healed?" Maggy asked.

Salter described the healing process:

> When wounded children and grownups arrive here they are bedded in tubs filled with healing waters. It is no easy work. The wounds have to be treated and their body has to be washed. Amputated limbs regrow within a short time and the sick tissue regenerates itself. Marie does all this work. She is a very resolute woman and has much help.

Salter added that many people on the third plane join in on the healing work. Everybody on the third plane has a task and working with the healing waters is one of these tasks.

Maggy contacted Juergen's mother, who confirmed that her son indeed had curly blonde hair and was friendly toward everyone, perhaps excessively. She burst into tears, saying that she had held her murdered boy in her arms, had seen the terrible stab wounds on his head. She said it helped her a great deal to know that Juergen was alive and had forgotten the horrible event.

Later, Salter contacted Maggy by phone, and Maggy heard the happy voices of many children playing, laughing, and singing; though some cried as adult voices tried to soothe them. Maggy asked "Where are you?"

Salter answered:

> I am bringing this communication from the children's home of Marie Mreches. There are many

such homes here in which children are looked after. Little babies are here, too. Many women and men are constantly taking care of the children. New children may be arriving at any time. Of course, not all of them are taken care of here.

It was hard to understand Salter because the children were so noisy. The voices of men and women were also heard in the background, loudly at times. Evidently, Timestream's voice modulating devices were working too well!

For those women and men who were unable to have children on Earth they are now able to be surrounded by children. And there is no shortage of children arriving. To Jules and Maggy, bringing the messages of children to their parents is the most rewarding part of their work.

As Jules said thoughtfully:

A few days ago, I asked myself, "Why are you doing all this? You have a good job, no problems. You could lead a carefree life, travel, be socially active and enjoy life. Instead, you sit at a desk every free minute, you work weekends and Sundays. You have no holidays and no vacation. And why? To be called weird, crazy or perhaps even a swindler or cheat. Is that what you really want?" Then I glanced at the front page of this issue [the CETL newsletter] with the smiling face of Ezra Braun. Thinking about my conversation with his father I knew that I was going to continue this work with all available means and strength. I would never get tired of passing along what was given to me: The message of eternal life and survival of personality and spirit.

To Jules, the endless conferences, the bickering of scientists, both pro and con, the constant need to document their research, the endless patience, the long sleepless hours, the people who know nothing of their research and who doubt Instrumental Transcommunication, do not make his life easy. But the children—they make it all worthwhile.

3

Forever Sweethearts—

JEANETTE AND GEORGE MEEK—LOVERS WHO WAIT FOR EACH OTHER

George Meek had always congratulated himself about his genuinely happy marriage. His wife Jeannette had not only been his sweetheart, but she'd shared his interest in psychology and parapsychology. George had done very well over the years as an international engineering consultant and they'd lived very comfortably. But now, she'd had a series of strokes and they both knew she was going to die. He understood death was only a transition into another life. But it was going to be very hard to be separated from her.

Suddenly, the time he'd been with her seemed so incredibly short. He thought back about his life. He'd always been an other-worldly man. From the moment he'd graduated from the University of Michigan in the summer of 1932 with an engineering degree, to the day he retired, he'd been fascinated with psychology and especially parapsychology. He knew that the part of the human being that can be seen and touched is but the tip of the iceberg, that man's basic nature lies beyond the physical world, beyond the scope of the five senses.

By the time he was sixty, he'd become a successful entrepreneur, inventor and globetrotter with a number of patents to his name. But in 1970, he decided to retire in order to pursue his life-long dream of learning all he could about man's basic nature. He had always been driven by a deep inner urge to figure out what makes things, and especially people, tick.

With ample savings after his retirement, George traveled extensively with Jeannette, visiting healers, inventors and researchers in dozens of countries. He had a free-wheeling way with his life savings. He gave money to struggling researchers and mediums, and he invited scientists, doctors and other experts along on many of his travels, paying all their expenses. Jeannette had been born with the name "Mary Jeannette Duncan," and she inherited all the thrift that her Scottish surname suggested. Jeannette Duncan Meek loved and needed security in her marriage. Sometimes, her frugality and her husband's generosity would rub up against each other, and there would be tension, a tension that seemed to provide a driving force for their marriage. Like Yin and Yang, or like shock absorbers and springs on a car, the Meeks' opposite natures had a stabilizing influence on the marriage.

George and Jeannette settled in Fort Myers, Florida, which quickly became her favorite place in the world. They had a lot of friends there. They owned a large houseboat and, maybe best of all, Jeannette could enjoy a refreshing swim every morning before breakfast. Some of their best years together were spent in Fort Myers.

Then they moved to North Carolina, and things were never quite the same for Jeannette. She had enjoyed a long swim every morning at their old home, but now there was nowhere to swim. They'd enjoyed close friendships among the vibrant Floridians, but making friends with the homespun, deeply rooted Smoky Hills folks took a great deal more time and effort. Jeannette loved George as much as ever, and she always seemed to sense that their love alone could get them through anything. But still, a small part of her couldn't seem to come to grips with their new life.

They took occasional trips to Florida to visit friends, and with every passing year, the return drive became more and more difficult for Jeannette. She tried to keep this little part of her tucked quietly inside, but apparently it was much stronger than she realized. On the way home from one visit in 1989, Jeannette suffered a massive stroke in the car.

In the spring of 1989, after a series of strokes, Jeannette lay on her deathbed. One part of her—the spiritual part—was ready for the new adventure about to begin, while her more down-to-earth part felt reluctant to leave George. Now, blind in one eye, and unable to speak or move, she discovered she could communicate with George telepathically through their psychically gifted housekeeper, Loree, who was a natural medium.

For months, George activated a tape recorder next to Jeannette's bed, and the two shared their innermost thoughts and feelings through Loree. They both knew Jeannette would make her transition soon, and that George would follow a few years later. They knew that they would then have a wonderful reunion in the spirit world. All of the research George had done during his life, his many meetings with para-psychologists and scientists working with spirit communication, had convinced him that he would be with her again.

Together, from their new home, a step or two closer to God, they would continue to help people still on Earth to find their spiritual way.

On the day before Jeannette's passage, George asked her to get firmly in mind two names: Timestream and Swejen Salter. He explained that Timestream was the name of a spirit-world sending station whose "staff" of over 1000 spirit beings were quickly mastering the art of sending long messages and clear video images to their colleagues on Earth through televisions, radios, computers, faxes, and telephones. Swejen Salter was the young woman who was the project leader at Timestream. Two decades of spiritual research told George that the two names, planted in Jeannette's mind, would act as a homing signal to pull Jeannette's spirit to the Timestream sending station.

The next day, in April of 1990, Jeannette died. George grieved at the loss of his sweetheart, but he waited patiently. Finally, his patience was rewarded. Three months after Jeannette's death, George received a letter from her which had been sent to CETL in

Luxembourg from Timestream. When Maggy and Jules discovered it on their computer's hard drive, they printed it on their printer and forwarded it to George in North Carolina. Jeannette, having worked with George over many years, and knowing his scientific mind, gave proofs of things only she and George knew:

Dear G.W.,

Well, it seems there are still people who do not believe in the contacts your friends here in Luxembourg are having. Hence, I will give you some personal details known only to you and Molly.

FIRST STORY. In 1987, end of April, our tenant Debbie called to say her refrigerator was off. It must have been on a Thursday morning

SECOND STORY. On April 29, 1987, Ann Valentin wrote a letter from California saying she had not received the *Magic of Living* booklets she had ordered, but instead had received a box of Harlequin novels.

THIRD STORY. John Lathrop shut off the electricity at our rental house to put in the new yard light. He wasn't down there very long but charged $20 service in addition to $40 for the bulbs, plus tax. The charge seemed high. Don't try to explain this, Honey. My never-ending love to you. I miss you so much, but I know we will be together.

Love forever ...Jeannette Duncan Meek

To validate the contact, Jeannette had selected three items known only to the Meeks and their assistant Molly Philo. The second item about romance novels, in fact, was a puzzle even to George. He had to call his old friend, Ann Valentin, to verify it. Of course, it checked out. Ann had received a box of Harlequin novels instead of the booklets she'd ordered. George remembered, too, the incident about John Lathrop. It had irked both him and Jeannette.

Meanwhile, Jeannette quickly settled into her new home. She took on a new assignment—receiving and comforting victims of the Persian Gulf crisis and helping them adjust. She learned from the Light Beings in the next dimension how to advance to higher spiritual dimensions, and she made new friends, including ragtime composer Scott Joplin.

Then in November 1992, the Luxembourg researchers received a computer-scanned image from their spirit colleagues, which was accompanied by the following computer text:

> Hello, my name is Hal Roach, and I am more than a hundred years old. I am at present a member of the artistic team of Timestream and am working together with old friends like George Cukor and others in the group of Klaus Schreiber and Eli Schaefer. This picture shows you a glimpse at the fourth level [astral dimension] as we see it.
>
> You can see Jeannette Meek and Nancy Carol coming through a dispassing point[1] in our level.
>
> Well, that should be enough for you folks for today. I am eager to learn more about this new world I'm living in now.
>
> Hal Roach 11-21-92, 7:54 (a.m.)

Hal Roach had been a well known producer of such television series as *Our Gang Comedy*. Nancy Carol, the young lady in a dark dress who appears next to Jeannette's face, astonished George. This was his

---

[1]A dispassing point is a place where dimensions cross.

daughter who had died at the age of two weeks. She was now a beautiful young woman. (See Plate 20)

In the many dialogues across dimensions, Jeannette told George how their daughter had grown quickly from infancy to young adulthood in the spirit world.

I [Mark Macy] have stayed in contact with Jeannette Meek as well. I often work with a gifted medium, Jean Peterson. In the summer of 1993, George and I asked Jean to channel information from Jeannette. The contact gave us much insight on her new life in spirit. Jeannette had been a warm, folksy woman, and still was in her new life as her own words reveal:

MARK: As I understand it, Jeannette, you have befriended Scott Joplin [black American composer].

JEANNETTE: Yes, we've been making a bit of music together, but don't tell George. I'm only kidding, honey.

MARK: (chuckles): Is he still involved in music in the plane where he is now?

JEANNETTE: Yes. Music being a universal language, music *is* in one's soul, an experience that continues.

MARK: From what I've discussed with George, you've been involved quite a bit with the Spiritual Hierarchy, and also you've had some brief meetings with Timestream. Can you tell me something about the group, and the occasion on which you transmitted your picture and computer letter?

JEANNETTE: Well, it's a matter of what you'd call working with energy—manipulating, controlling and directing energy in such a way that it aligns with wherever the energy is that you're sending. It does no good if one wants to send a thought in your world to Moscow if someone is unable to receive the thought by mental telepathy. So you have another method of getting the message through. You can write, or you can have a friend who's traveling there deliver the message to a person on that end, or you can use the telephone. It's a matter of understanding what you want to accomplish and how to do it.

Now I know how to send thoughts telepathically to your dimension from where I am. It's a matter of reception on the other end. How is it that I can send my picture and thoughts so that they will be received by a certain group of people? I send them to Timestream from where I am. For the Timestream group there is a way to transfer these things to Earth. There's more than one way. So for my part, I tune into the energy of Timestream—I know how to do it—and I get the job done.

MARK: When you were in the Timestream sending station, located in the astral planes, who were you working with?

JEANNETTE: You understand that there are technicians and people who are here. When a person wants to send some thoughts or a picture or whatever, you just send yourself through what you would think of as thought or desire. Let's call it desire to create this thing, and you know how to do it, in the same way that you would go to the telephone and you have to know a certain number to reach a certain person. I do a similar thing here, and I'm working with whoever is working at Timestream at the moment of transmission.

The Timestream sending station is not what you would think of as a place. It is a vibration that one can touch.

MARK: Were you involved in materializing the actual picture of you that was sent?

JEANNETTE: I posed, you might say, but it would not be with a camera. It would be energy transmission.

MARK: Is Nancy Carol still spending time or sharing efforts with you?

JEANNETTE: Not so much as in the beginning. She has developed in other directions, and she comes and goes, as grown up children do in Earth life.

MARK: What is she doing now?

JEANNETTE: She's working on some projects with some friends of hers. She's been working, believe it or not, with the soul of a little dog. And she's been doing some projects like what you'd call "cooking up" some things. She's been working on a personal energy connection with another soul. She's doing some work with water. She's also been deciding whether she'd like to reincarnate to Earth.

MARK: Oh. Is she leaning in that direction?

JEANNETTE: The thought comes and goes. She was thinking of living near the ocean.

MARK: Don't you have a lot of oceans where you are?

JEANNETTE: We have everything you could imagine. It's just unlimited, whatever you want to experience. But yes, she's been thinking about reincarnation again on Earth. (pause) I understand what you're asking. It is that this soul who was my daughter on Earth is a vast entity that is so far beyond in her understanding, beyond the portion of her soul that occupied that tiny infant body; I not only see that part and can communicate that part with George, but I can perceive and interact with the total soul. We need not limit each other to where we have to spend vast amounts of time together as a mother and daughter on Earth might do. Do you understand?

MARK: Yes. In fact, I was wondering, when you crossed over initially and met Nancy Carol as an infant, I wonder if she was an infant at that time because you wanted her to be, and then she grew up quickly . . . .

JEANNETTE: Her being an infant was a means of recognition. It's not like on Earth where it takes time for a person to evolve from infancy to adulthood; here it can be experienced at any moment. Any memory a soul contains can be relived. So it was just a means of memory connection, of recognition, that she connected with me as my infant daughter.

MARK: Do many situations occur in which a person crosses over and they feel so uncomfortable and out of place that things are made to accommodate them, to make them feel more comfortable?

JEANNETTE: The newcomers make those accommodations for themselves, sometimes with assistance from friends. There is an order to Heaven. And there is an order to the memory and to the reconnecting with the higher vibrations to make things comfortable, or familiar, for ourselves. So at any moment I could have touched in with Nancy Carol's energy as the infant I remembered and at any moment decide which part of her soul I would interact with in the next moment.

MARK: Are you on what George would call the Celestial Plane, or do you even consider that sort of terminology?

JEANNETTE: Oh, we do. Yes. Various beings define it in different ways. I am able to travel as far as my frequency has developed. In your understanding, I could come and go even to the Ascended Master level, what George calls the Celestial Plane. But I do not stay in that frequency for long periods of time.

MARK: Where do you feel most comfortable?

JEANNETTE: What you would call a home space, what you would call a frequency of love, the understanding of love and oneness.

MARK: I hope I can meet you eventually in a manner in which I can see or feel your energy as well.

JEANNETTE: Yes, well, if you get on with this writing.

MARK: Automatic writing, you're referring to?

JEANNETTE: We're talking about telepathic communication.

MARK: That is certainly my aim. Do you have any tips? The channel [Jean] has loaned me a copy of *The Dynamics of Cosmic Telepathy*, by Tuella. Any other ideas?

JEANNETTE: Create a small amount of time regularly—once a week or once a day—when you can do your meditation to align yourself, state your desire, and write. The book by Tuella will help. Now, as we've said, there are no magic wands, so when you wish to develop this telepathy you put in some physical energy because you are on a physical plane. And the recognition, the higher-frequency energy, comes through the physical. So when that is aligned, when the desire is stated, and when the will to produce emerges, the recognition of it will come. I, along with others, will work with you as we work with George and others. Anyway, you do some channeled writing frequently; you just may not be aware of it.

MARK: Thank you! Since we are still in contact, when I work with George—this is something that is important to me right now—how do you view my work with George? Do you see it evolving in a positive way?

JEANNETTE: Yes, through the contacts you are being led toward and through your own desire for service in your own way. You will produce works that will be of assistance in raising consciousness through your writing, through one-on-one, group communication, film and through your teaching skills. That contact with George is leading to more and more energy connections around the planet.

From our perspective, the foundation of George's work has its own solid structure, but you will take that foundation and build your own building, so to speak, and create your own destiny. That foundation will be a springboard to the continuation of George's work, but at the same time the building is your own creation. What we attempt to do from these levels, while tying the dimensions together, is to have a continuing work with Earth. And, so, just as a father in your dimension hopefully passes on a family business to a son, George's hopes and ours, too, is that this foundation will continue with the structure which you have built upon it. How those energies tie together and continue is a beautiful thing to see from our level. We would encourage you to continue with your own building.

MARK: I appreciate that very much.

JEANNETTE: So the apple, then, has seeds. The person eats the apple, enjoys it and throws the core to the Earth, and it's entirely possible that an entire tree can spring up from what some would consider waste or litter. So it is with George's work and how you would take those seeds and grow an even greater abundance than George has been able to do in his time.

MARK: There seems to be a lot of fertile soil for it to take root now, the way the world is today.

JEANNETTE: That's right, it's timing that allows a tree to grow.

About six months after our dialogue with Jeannette, I [Mark] was part of one of the first planned telephone communications with Timestream to the United States. I received a telephone call on January 21, 1994, from Dr. Konstantin Raudive. It was so unexpected, I was not prepared with a tape recorder. Konstantin said this contact was a historic moment. You can imagine how frustrated I was, not to be able to record that historic conversation.

However, Konstantin also called George Meek; and George was prepared! The date was January 27, 1994, when the phone rang. George felt the flare of excitement when he realized it was Konstantin Raudive. He was intimately familiar with the work of electronic voice pioneer Dr. Raudive, *who had died in 1974!* Ordinarily George might have been a bit suspicious, but I had called him a week earlier and told him of my phone contact with Raudive. What he then heard was to be the first taped telephone conversation from the astral plane to the United States.

GEORGE: Hello, this is George Meek.

RAUDIVE (in a very deep voice, speaking slowly, carefully, with hints of a Northern European accent): This is Konstantin Raudive. George, my friend, at last we have succeeded in contacting you. Jeannette is beside me, and she wants to give you all her love. I suppose that you can hear me?

GEORGE: I can hear you very well, very plainly.

RAUDIVE: Fine, so this is the first contact you get from us. This is the beginning of a new story, a new chapter, George. You are a very good friend of ours, even if we haven't met. This is the first bridge we have succeeded in building to the States. Mark was contacted, and I must interrupt now. This is Konstantin Raudive.

Since his death in 1974, Konstantin Raudive has been helping his colleagues on Earth to make ITC a success. He says it is his calling. It appears to be the calling of George and Jeannette Meek as well. Jeannette is already keeping in close touch with Timestream and with her husband during his final years on Earth. George is looking forward to his coming reunion with Jeannette and the projects he can do once he is young again, with boundless energy. George says he is eager to do what he can to open up communication between two worlds.

4

The Third Plane—

WHAT IT'S LIKE TO LIVE IN
A NEW DIMENSION

From 1986 to 1993, fifty different male and female voices have spoken through the technical equipment at Luxembourg. All of them described landscapes on the third (mid-astral) plane that reminded them of Earth. Fog, night, rivers, lakes, stars, mountains and polar caps are all part of the landscape. Any type of house the mind can imagine is here: houses with thatched roofs, magnificent palaces with glass towers and roofs of gold.

One man, a vine grower, joyfully remarked that he had a vineyard in the spirit world and that his grapes were more beautiful than he'd ever seen. Other spirits spoke of rivers and mountains that reminded them of Earth, but couldn't fit them into any particular Earth locale. Most of them said they were aware they had "passed over" to this new locale, but they couldn't remember how they'd gotten here.

The "here" is the planet Marduk, not in the Earth's solar system. It has three suns. The planet orbits one sun and is illuminated by the other two. It is never totally dark. The circumference of Marduk is approximately 127,000 kilometers. Marduk has a moon larger than Earth's moon. A single large river, The River of Eternity, flows across the entire planet. The deepest part of the river is 17,000 kilometers and the widest spot is 3700 kilometers. Scattered along this river are sixty billion people.

The landscape is not continually shifting and changing; there are certain constants. Cities exist, as do schools and universities. Today, such descriptions of the astral planes are not uncommon as countless people have near-death experiences (NDEs) and out-of-body experiences (OBEs) and report them either in private to family and close friends, or publicly through articles, books and lectures. Robert Monroe, former TV executive and now Director of the Monroe Institute of Applied Science in Virginia, has had innumerable out-of-body trips and he claims that he is at present mapping the astral plane. He says that he has trained fifty students to astral project as a group to given points on the astral plane.

Monroe, a pioneer in astral travel, has written several books on astral projection[1] and is internationally known for his work on the effects of sound wave forms on human behavior. Many of his students, highly respected engineers, physicists, doctors, teachers, psychiatrists and social service workers come to Virginia to study out-of-body techniques.

Swejen Salter, Director of Timestream, describes the River of Eternity as the astral plane's main

---

[1]Monroe's books are: *Journeys out of the Body, Far Journeys*, and *Ultimate Journey*.

topographical feature and says it winds like a snake around the entire planet of Marduk and that it seems to be fed by tributaries which originate in the surrounding mountains.

She says there appears to be a different kind of physics here. A river of this kind is impossible from a physics perspective on Earth, that is, the existence of a single river which encircles the entire planet. The ground has no layers here, as on Earth, and there seems to be no water seepage.

Whole communities are clumped along the river, communities of people who lived many years ago, such as the ancient Vikings and people of the Stone Age. They wear the same clothes they wore then. A history buff has the opportunity to study different periods of history and to talk to the people who lived during those periods. In fact, a deceased French scientist named Rimbaud is living with people of the early Stone Age to study their habits.

Along the river, too, are communities of people where everyone is of a particular religion, particular nationality, or had the same cultural or sports interests. Catholics, Protestants and those of other faiths may remain segregated, secure in their particular beliefs. However, as people live on this plane, feelings of divisiveness between the various groups begin to fade. They begin to feel at home with others of all races and beliefs.

Life is safe and secure here, free of any misery and suffering. And some people have lived here for hundreds of years without reincarnating. But gradually, each person becomes aware of the things he did not finish or learn on Earth and the time comes when a person wants to progress, to learn new things.

Then it is time to make a "reality change" or what we call "reincarnate." For whatever one did not learn on Earth, whatever life lessons one evaded, those things will hold one back from progressing to higher planes of existence.

The point is that one can create many mental constructs and play with ideas on the astral plane. But actually living on Earth is putting one's ideas into nitty gritty practice. Life is the acid test of what a person really believes in. For example, here on Earth, Mother Teresa is not simply visualizing taking care of the sick. She *is* taking care of the sick in a physically demanding situation and she is using her life energy to do it.

One of the purposes of the astral plane is to wean humans away from patriotism and nationalism. On the higher planes there is a universal understanding. There is no separation by time, space or dimension. Each soul is part of the whole.

Timestream gives an analogy of a crystal to illustrate the point:

> ...assume all positive and negative thoughts, intentions and actions could come together and form a huge crystal. On the outside, the crystal could be surrounded by rough stone but on the inside it would glow in the most beautiful colors and its center would contain all our souls. The illumination of this great soul would penetrate, step by step, the irregularities of its rough surrounding. The beauty of the crystal would become more visible every day. Now realize that the core of this shiny crystal contains the spiritual potential of all of us, including those of different eras of time and of different origin.

New arrivals in spirit often join the nationality group closest to the roots of their origin and they receive the living quarters they ask for, although some join already established spirit families. In general, one turns toward those groups that share one's interest. So there are communities of artists and musicians as well.

A first encounter with third plane inhabitants may be with people from past time history or with an intelligent being who looks entirely different than we do on Earth. The ability to be flexible and to accept the new and unusual, leads one toward progressively new dimensions.

Death is a great adventure. The newly deceased, after a short rest period of a few days or weeks, may decide to travel on the third plane and see the sights. Or they may be very happy to be reunited with old friends and relatives on the astral plane. They may even meet relatives they never really got to know on Earth. After death, the entire memory of the individual's past lives is restored and he or she may even seek out friends and relatives of a former past life shared in some long ago past time. As spirit researcher Friedrich Juergenson said in a computer contact in 1992, "Beings keep their individuality during 'reality changes' with their consciousness and reincarnations."

The new world is a world of discovery. Sometimes, these meetings with friends and relatives are exciting or sometimes one realizes that there is nothing in common at all and so one moves on to develop new relationships.

Some of the inhabitants on the third plane still are interested in what's happening on Earth and others couldn't care less. Konstantin Raudive's wife, Zenta Marina, resides on the fourth plane. She has no interest in Earth or even to live on the third plane because they both remind her of the long illnesses of her Earthly life.

Her husband, Konstantin, moves freely between the fourth plane, where he still enjoys his wife's company, and the third plane where he works on the communication program at Timestream.

When a person lives on a higher plane he also has the ability to move into a lower plane and to construct a body that will function on that plane.

Yogis explain that, similarly, Christ and the masters can freely ascend and descend through the planes at will and can visit Earth at any time.

One of the main tasks on the third plane is to locate those lost souls who are entitled to live on this plane but who for some reason or other have not yet found their way here. Some people do not even realize they have died, and some have rejected the idea of life after death or have not even considered it. After death, these people remain in a confused state wandering around in their homes and among their friends, and it is hard to reach them. People who have died violent deaths also remain in a confused state for awhile, around the scene of their murder or accident, and are still reliving their battles in their mind.

As the third plane is a construct of the mind, the soldier killed on the battlefield may well awaken in a battle scene, the world of his thoughts.

These thoughts of fear and confusion reach Timestream as energy vibrations and, as there is the possibility that the newly arrived dead person may not find his or her way to the new world, actual search parties are sent out to find the person and escort him to the third plane.

Robert Monroe also speaks of the rescue function and remarks that he has rescued people and taken them to their proper destination on the third plane.

Besides the main task of locating the newly dead, many people can journey around the planet Marduk as well as travel to the stars. They also make their way along the River of Eternity by both mechanical conveyances and the power of thought alone.

Swejen Salter says that she and Richard Francis Burton were traveling along the river, five years ago, when they discovered the Timestream Lab. It seemed to be waiting for them. She and Sir Richard feel that the Technician and the higher entities who work with them now are not yet ready to reveal the entirety of the mission. The founding of Timestream Lab is a "preparation phase" which may extend over thousands of Earth-time years.

Salter and Sir Richard have been told that Marduk is in another galaxy, Spiral Galaxy NGC4866, and that it doesn't exist in a physical four-dimensional plane.

Salter compares Timestream lab in size to a huge post office or a very busy bank building. She says there is no technical space program here such as on Earth:

> There are totally different possibilities open to us. We can travel in space mentally and with our mind visit other dimensions and other planets to explore them. However, it is possible here to travel with the help of large dirigible blimps or hot air balloons. There are aircraft—small two seaters which are used by airplane enthusiasts. Many people use ziolcopters here. They are similar to helicopters but fly according to a different physical principle, and therefore their technical construction is different than their counterpart on Earth. There is also

surface travel here mainly in electrical automobiles
and solar-powered vehicles.

When the experimenters asked Timestream why
mechanical conveyances were used when third plane
inhabitants could travel by the power of their mind
alone, Timestream replied that people "liked" cars and
airplanes. They construct the vehicles they like.
Similarly, although it is not necessary to eat here,
people enjoy eating with their friends and create the
food they like.

Mark Macy says that spirit researcher Klaus
Schreiber had a brother (living on Earth) who was a
motorcycle buff. The boy was killed in a motorcycle
accident. Now, he still rides motorcycles but he
travels at incredible speeds that are inconceivable on
Earth.

Salter goes on to say that because she can enter into
the fourth plane, she can transfer herself mentally to
other realities and contact entities of other dimensions
while remaining on the third plane. She remarks that
Richard often travels to other planets to get to know
the inhabitants there. These trips are not comparable
to space travel done on Earth as far as space and time
are concerned. His trips to other planets seem to him
to be a "day-long experience," but Salter says that to
her it seems he is only away for a few minutes.

Salter says that she has made long journeys with the
help of a transmitter capsule. The astral body is
dematerialized, dissolved into matter much finer than
atoms. She floated in space and felt very well. Only
the journey took as long as it would in the physical
body when traveling by ship on a river or by air.

She tells of the beautiful, spacious home she and Sir
Richard share. In Earth terms, it's about 4,350 square

feet and is similar to a rented apartment. It opens many dimensions to them because their life is not limited by space or time. She is able to walk through the back door of the apartment into an absolutely immense, beautiful garden. Everything looks as real to her as our world looks to us.

Just by walking through her back door, she is also able to visit exotic parks, stroll on beautiful beaches, or admire a sunset over the ocean.

An Earthside researcher commented that her world is "an illusion of the mind." To which Salter replied, "That is correct." But to her, it is reality and she has the opportunity to see many worlds. As she says: "I only see things that exist."

She counters that, on Earth too, a car and the most beautiful house in the world are also illusions of the mind. Only on the third plane, things can be mentally constructed much more quickly than we on Earth can build them.

The Indian yogi, Paramahansa Yogananda, once commented that while he could "think a book" almost instantaneously on the astral plane, it would take him a whole year to write the book in Earth time.

Many of our departed relatives, friends, and also beings of different eras and cultures live on Marduk. Most of us on Earth have a large spiritual family in the spirit world and while we may not be aware of these family members, they often intercede for us and support us from the other side. Many of these spirit brothers and sisters shared earlier Earth lives with us and have not reincarnated since. When we finally pass over into the spirit world, they are waiting for us.

We may not remember them immediately, but they know a great deal about us. They are linked to our very soul.

Soul relationships exist beyond time and space. Sometimes, on Earth, even though a soul is bonded to another soul, they are separated from each other because one has a particular task on Earth that must be carried out.

Just as our spirit relatives wait for us, so often do our family pets—if a bond of love has been formed. Pets are often taken in by our spirit relatives and if the pet wishes to see us that wish is granted. In the spirit world there is a grand reunion between the newly deceased and those little animal souls who have waited patiently, perhaps for years.

Here on the third plane one may meet the enemy one fought on a battlefield. Spirits from older times, as well as contemporary, want us to understand that no matter why they fought, each believed in the rightness of the cause.

Sometimes, for many people, waking up in the next world is a crushing shock. Few people find that the third plane corresponds with their expectations. As on Earth, they discover that among the inhabitants here are petty thieves, fraudulent businessmen, pickpockets, adulterers, and liars. These types are separated into their own respective groups and cannot hurt the more respectable spirits. But many souls wonder why they have to live in the same dimension with them instead of being in the promised paradise.

But Salter reminds: "Our dimension is neither heaven nor hell."

Again, the third plane is not a "permanent place." It is only an interim place until the soul either reincarnates back to Earth, moves on to another planet, or proceeds through an evolutionary process up into the fourth plane or maybe even into the celestial planes nearer to God.

Spirit researcher Friedrich Juergenson in his computer contacts says:

> ...it is "idle speculation" to theorize what waits for you on the other side, on the third plane. If you didn't solve your problems on Earth, they will be waiting for you here. In this new reality, the titles and positions held on Earth are unimportant. What remains is *your soul*. What is really important here are your ethical feelings and the humanities, all things of a constructive nature.
>
> Some people want to look for new ways and others want to preserve old values and add new knowledge. Here, on the third plane, the field is wide open to you. All possibilities are also realities. There is total freedom and total choice.

As part of the Timestream communication team, Juergenson says:

> Our message is to tell you that your life goes on. Any speculations how an individual will experience it are bound to be limited in validity. All your scientific, medical, or biological speculations miss the mark of these realities. What serves as "real" to science is not close to reality in the broad picture. It is no more than a word out of a book.

He emphasizes that each person has his or her responsibility with "thought power." Negative thoughts create negative realities and positive, constructive thoughts create positive, constructive realities. We are always creating our own environment through thought. Our mental attitude about life is creating our spiritual environment right now. We are responsible for the environment we will go to after death.

"Thoughts have no limits!" says Juergenson. They reach across all dimensions.

There's no escape from the consequences of your thoughts and actions. You cannot expect to live in a better world if you act and think negatively. When the physical body disintegrates, your astral body, which contains your thoughts, emotions and memories, is released to live on the astral plane. It is up to you whether you live on the lower planes of darkness and pain, the higher astral planes of beauty and love, or the even higher planes of the celestial beings closest to God. *It's your choice.* Every moment on Earth, the choices you make here, determine your afterlife.

5

Jacob's Ladder—

A MULTIDIMENSIONAL UNIVERSE ACCORDING TO INSTRUMENTAL TRANSCOMMUNICATION [ITC] RESEARCHERS

One scenario of our fleeting lives on planet Earth is to live a long life, and at the end of that life we tell our loved ones who are gathered around our deathbed, "Why, I've lived to be ninety. Do you know how much I did during my life-time?" Then we die. Suddenly, we wake up in another place and ask, "How long was I gone?" The Being of Light who is with us replies, "We hardly noticed you were gone at all. You just sat down and dozed off for a moment, and here you are again. Let's see what kind of dreams you had this time."

What part of us "wakes up" after we die? And where exactly do we find ourselves when we "wake up?" These questions, probably more so than any others, have baffled and preoccupied our ancestors down through the ages.

Early religions and philosophies produced some rather elaborate scenarios of the postmortem experience which satisfied people's curiosities quite well, thank you...until the knowledge gathered by modern sciences and parasciences [especially facts about electromagnetic and etheric energies] began falling into place like puzzle pieces. Today, due to ITC, we have a much clearer picture of what life is really like after we shed the physical body.

Some of the questions ITC researchers and their invisible colleagues in the subtler dimensions have answered is:

Do we have a soul?

Is there a God?

Is there a "heaven" where most of us wind up after we die?

Is there a "hell"?

Is there a "Devil"?

What exactly will life be like after we die?

Does everyone reincarnate?

OUR MULTI-DIMENSIONAL BODY

Deceased scientists who now live in the next dimension say that we indeed do have a soul. They describe it as a small beam of undying Light which resides in the area of the heart. Curiously, the ancient yogis spoke of the soul, calling it the "seed atom" and said it resided in the left ventricle of the heart. Today's research seems to validate the yogic concept.

Imagine yourself a video illustrator for a moment, preparing to animate a sequence of pictures that show the soul evolving into a human body. This sequence involves five basic stages, each of which melts or merges into the next:

In Stage One, we see the soul, a small beam of light.

In Stage Two, a ball of energy emanates from the soul, surrounding it like a cloud. Now the soul is called a "Light Being" and its energies are very fine, very subtle. This being operates on a very high frequency, on what is called the mental-causal plane.

In Stage Three, the astral body is formed. The vibrations become heavier and the Light Being begins to assume a shape similar to the physical body. Still it is composed of a substance lighter and finer than that of the physical body. It is so light and wispy that it hardly exists at all. It consists of energy cells instead of living body cells and is called the "Astral Body" or the "Energy Body" and it resides on what is called the astral plane.

In Stage Four, the vibrations become heavier and the body now becomes denser than the astral body and even more closely resembles the physical body. In this fourth stage of manifestation, the body is referred to as the "etheric body." Sometimes, it's also called the "electrical Body" and Russian scientists referred to it as the "beta Body" or "bioplasmic Body" in their experiments with the auric field (a body of energy that surrounds the physical body). The etheric body is invisible to the average person, but many psychics are able to see it.

In Stage Five, the last stage, the physical body comes into form. Now, matter is vibrating at its lowest speed, and is at its densest stage. The physical body lives on the physical plane where we are now and can be perceived by the five senses. All of our other bodies are invisible to us unless we are clairvoyant or developed psychically.

Each body is able to function on its own plane or dimension and if one is developed psychically one can travel to the lower planes. To travel to the celestial planes, spiritual development is needed.

Reversing the stages is called Death. For death is the process of the soul returning to its natural state. The eternal soul sheds its physical body, sheds its etheric body, its astral and mental body, moving back through the planes, toward the Light, and if it has completed its evolution, it returns to the Source of Light—the Creator.

But not every soul returns to the Source, or the Creator, until it is ready. Each soul has its own path of evolution, its own inner direction, and also its own free will. Each soul marches to the music of its own inner drummer.

Man, then, is a multidimensional being and has many bodies—not only a physical body, perceived through the five senses, but also the etheric, the astral, and the mental/causal, which have emanated from the Soul, a tiny beam of light.

You are all these things now. That is the key to spiritual understanding. When you die, you shed the physical body and begin the voyage home, through the planes. As Christ said: "In my Father's house are many mansions" or *dimensions*.

When you die, for a short period of time, you will probably remain in the same vicinity where you died, or in the home where you spent many years. You will have the experience of seeing your friends and loved ones, but unless they are clairvoyant they will not see you. Though they may sense your presence. You will definitely feel frustrated when you talk to them and they don't answer. And you may tap them on the shoulder only to find that your hand goes through them. (See Plate 21)

Still, despite this frustration, you will feel wonderful, amazingly light and free. Living in the physical world is like carrying a heavy weight around, a heavy suit of armor. You will discover that you have 360 degree vision, that your body has limited your vision. Being in this "dead" state seems natural, not frightening. It is very possible that you will not be interested in your dead body, that you have never felt more alive. You may even wonder why people are so interested in that dead body and are crying when you happen to be standing right there. You will notice that your aches and pains have vanished. And it is very probable you will attend your own funeral and listen to your own eulogy. Now, mixing with your friends and relatives, you will begin to realize what others really thought of you and you will feel a curious detachment about the person you once were.

Some years ago, I [Pat Kubis] experienced my first out of body state at Hollywood High School in my freshman year. I fainted in the gym and my body slid under a table. Suddenly, I found myself floating above my body—a vast invisible creature, like a genie just released from a bottle. The gym had been prepared for graduation and it was full of flowers and the fragrance was overpowering, particularly the gladiolus. I delightedly discovered that I could see through walls, into the locker area and listen to the people laughing and joking.

I could also look through the table and see my body below. Then I noticed a group of teachers walking toward me. When they saw me, they pulled me out from the table and put me in a chair. Several of them ran for wet cloths to put on my face. Frankly, I didn't care about my body at all. I was so delighted about being free. When the teachers returned with the wet cloths, they began to wipe my face and I felt a strange pulling sensation, like the pulling of a strand of a spider web, and I realized I had to return to "that body." I really didn't want to go back into it. But then, I began to funnel back into my body and I opened my eyes regretfully. What marvelous freedom I had experienced!

Only later, when I went to college and took Comparative Literature did I realize that the Arabs (the Sufis) knew perfectly well about the astral body and that their tales about the "genie" were parables about the astral body.

One of our ITC colleagues (on Earth), Jean Peterson, makes etheric journeys frequently in her meditations and channeling work, and she equates physical life with "walking in Jello." She describes this life on Earth as very cumbersome. Death is really a liberation from a very uncomfortable state of being.

Our spirit colleagues describe the process of transition, saying:

> 1. After shedding the physical body, you live for a few days in a body of etheric energy, but then, that body, too, disintegrates.

> 2. Now you begin the journey to the next life on the astral plane. You may fall into a deep sleep for a few days or weeks during this transition. Although it is also possible to make the transition fully conscious and many advanced souls do.

> 3. You may waken in a hospital and find yourself being cared for by loving beings (provided you

have succeeded in reaching the middle or higher astral planes).

4. Deceased family members both from this time period and those from former lifetimes greet you.

5. Gradually, you discover you do not have to be old, ill, or decrepit. You see how young most of the people around you look (even your deceased grandmother) and you discover that you can choose to be the age at which you feel and look best.

6. Upon leaving the hospital, you notice that the environment is similar to that on Earth, only the colors are vivid and iridescent. There are beautiful gardens with flowers that do not decay and lovely birds with luminous foliage. To your immense joy, you discover that you can replicate objects on earth that you knew and loved.

But not every plane is beautiful or nurturing. A small percentage of people don't get as far as the mid-astral planes. They are trapped for a time in the lower astral planes, a dark, dismal place. This is the realm that inspired western world concepts of *hell and purgatory*. However, no one stays here permanently. At any given time, a person entrapped here may call for help and rescuers await to release the person from bondage.

WHO OR WHAT DETERMINES WHERE WE WILL WIND UP?

Interestingly enough, in all the data from Time-stream, there is no mention of a "Devil," or God sentencing anyone to the lower planes. Rather, man sentences himself by his own desires. What he *deeply desires or wants* acts as a magnetic attraction, attracting him to a plane where those things exist. In other words, it is our thoughts, attitudes, beliefs and behavior that raise or lower the frequency of our astral body, and when we die we simply go to the dimension that is compatible with our spirit.

Factors that raise the frequency of our astral body while we are alive on earth are:

1. Love
2. Compassion
3. Service to others
4. An air of calm detachment
5. Eating fresh fruits and vegetables
6. Drinking pure water and breathing clean air.
7. A realistic concept of spiritual existence.

Factors that lower our vibration or frequency are:

1. Fear
2. Hatred
3. Resentment
4. Egotism and selfishness
5. Attachment to worldly things
6. Using alcohol, tobacco and drugs regularly
7. Eating "heavy" foods such as red meat and fat
8. Hurting other people or animals with malicious intent
9. Spiritual ignorance or major misunderstanding

Our spirit colleagues warn that any combination of these things in excess can chain you to a lower plane. And, in the words of the poet, love can set you free.

Today, as one might guess, there is an over-population in the lower astral realms. Many people's lives revolve around negative thoughts, habits and activities that are harmful to the spirit.

If a person continues to think negatively, even in the afterdeath state, that person will almost certainly find himself or herself in the unsettling reaches of the lower astral plane.

The principal role of ITC in today's world is to promote spiritual growth of all people, first, by convincing even the most stubborn skeptics that life does indeed continue after we shed the physical body, and second, to show us all, through televised images and long messages on the computer hard drive, just what our next life will be like.

Hopefully, this knowledge will automatically direct our lives onto a more spiritual path. As the planes reveal, there are consequences to our actions.

Describing the higher spiritual dimensions is not possible in any great detail because they are far beyond our comprehension in their complexity and scope. Plate 23 gives a general idea of what these other worlds are like. They are based largely on the information we have received from our ITC colleagues in spirit.

The lower astral planes are a dark, dismal world. Some people, after dying, are magnetically pulled here by their low-vibration thoughts and attitudes. This region exists near the physical plane and it is chaotic. There is no time, space, or gravity in the spiritual world, and those beings trapped here live in a state of confusion. They may reside in this bewildering reality for years or for centuries of Earth time. Some are not even aware they are dead.

Many of the spirits in the lower astral planes cause a great deal of trouble on Earth. They can communicate telepathically to others on Earth and inspire weaker people, who think these thoughts are their own, to act badly. For example, spirits of deceased alcoholics, drug addicts, murderers and other violent criminals, are drawn to people on Earth who have a similar disposition or to people of a weaker will and the spirits encourage the vices to which they are addicted. These negative entities fuel negative thoughts, attitudes and behavior in people on Earth whose lives they have entered.

The middle astral planes are a pleasant realm where most of us wake up to be rehabilitated after our Earthly education—a school of hard knocks meant to develop our character and persistence.

The Timestream sending station and other spirit groups of ITC colleagues all convey their messages and images to Earth from the mid-astral planes. They describe concert halls, museums, hospitals, schools and homes much like those on Earth and set in landscapes of trees, flowers, mountains, meadows and rivers that, again, are like landscapes here on Earth, only much more breathtaking.

The third plane is an interim plane where we make a decision to move on to a higher plane or return to Earth for more experiential living.

The higher astral planes are a wonderful realm called Heaven by Christians, or the Summerland by spiritualists. Many of the spirit colleagues of ITC experimenters reside in the higher astral planes and "descend," or lower their vibratory rate, into the mid-astral planes in order to participate in ITC.

The mental-causal planes are realms of divine inspiration free of Earthly desires and conflict. The beings here cause many of the artistic and technical breakthroughs on Earth by sending telepathic messages to artists and inventors. A number of Light

Beings whose home frequencies are in the mental-causal planes assist the ITC projects by providing inspiration and guidance. They send messages of love and wisdom to the project leaders at Timestream, to be relayed to Earth.

One such being is the spirit of a girl named Angie Mreches (see Plate 23), granddaughter of Marie Mreches (see Chapter 3), who died at age twelve. As a child, she had been a special soul. The only blonde, blue-eyed member of a family of dark-haired people, Angie was a sensitive child. Our spirit colleagues have told us that Angie did not belong to the human line of evolution:

> She is in a line of nonhuman beings who incarnate in a human body or show themselves in body on the physical plane. The human body plays only a minor part for them. They accept it because it allows them to get to know us better and to study mankind much better. All information such an entity gains about human existence is automatically transferred to other beings of its kind. Angie remembers little of her years on Earth. Her years of incarnation were of minor importance to her.

Angie apparently acted as a communicating instrument meant to gather information for her non-human people. Her early death may explain the death of some children who do not need to learn all of life's lessons. (See Plate 24)

The Celestial Planes are the home of various Earth gods and deities whose wisdom, understanding and unconditionally loving nature are beyond human comprehension. One of these beings is Jesus Christ, or Yeshua Ben Yussuf, and the Technician says of Him:

> Yeshua Ben Yussuf belongs to the extremely high beings who are in direct contact with the Principle

whom men call God. The word "hierarchy" is a human expression. In the spirit world all higher beings are one and can fuse together into the Light. Man needs the image of certain beings as more spiritually advanced than others. It helps his understanding and assures a certain order. Higher beings are not dependent on the steps or divisions of a hierarchy. Yeshua, during His incarnation, tried to explain everything to the people as accurately as possible. Much of what He said they did not understand.

The Technician goes on to say that higher beings certainly do not want to experience such suffering as Yeshua experienced on Earth, but sometimes it is unavoidable. When Yeshua died during the crucifixion, he went directly into the celestial planes whereas most people stay in the astral planes. Mohammed, the Buddha, and other great teachers also moved to higher levels after they died. (See Plate 22)

These great spiritual teachers and many great personalities who are part of Earth's history, are incarnations of spirit beings from higher spheres. And the religions they founded, Buddhism, Confucianism, Taoism, Shinto, Islam, Judaism, Catholicism and Protestantism are all signposts to a higher purpose.

The Bible refers to the planes metaphorically as "Jacob's Ladder." Jacob had a vision and saw angels coming down and going up a ladder of light. In a sense we are like those angels. When we die the soul is released from its dense physical body and it journeys back through the planes to its spiritual home, and after a time it journeys back down the ladder of vibration to live again.

6

Reincarnation & the Consequences of Abortion

Jacob's vision of angels descending to Earth and then ascending to heaven again on a ladder of light may be the first accounting of reincarnation in Western Literature. For in a sense we are all angels, creatures created by God and composed of His essence, and we come to Earth and live here awhile and return to a world beyond.

Many religions have spoke of reincarnation and many books have been written on the subject, and in the conversations with our colleagues on the astral plane they too speak of reincarnation as part of the path of evolution. However, their viewpoint on reincarnation is now seen in a broader 20th century perspective, in the framework of a multi-dimensional universe.

The Technician, a Light Being from a higher plane and mentor of Timestream Lab says, "Reincarnation is a Spiritual Law." But he adds that every being here on Earth and in higher dimensions can "detour" this law for awhile to avoid it or even reject it, but it cannot be escaped forever.

The spirit scientists speak of a multi-dimensional universe with many planets and galaxies and they indicate that when we are in our spiritual bodies we are space travelers, able to visit and even live on many other planets. Evolution of the spirit demands a large universe.

Think of the immensity of this concept! The Earth is an average planet in a galaxy which contains 100 billion other stars and is further surrounded by 100 billion other galaxies.

Often we repeat spiritual concepts without perception—ideas such as "Life is Eternal." Yet eternal life to many religious people becomes a simplistic conclusion. Some of us believe that at the moment of death we are swept up to heaven and there we live in the city of God, and some even think we play harps perpetually. Yet common sense should step in and suggest that not everyone wants to play a harp and that to non-musicians such an existence would be a bloody bore.

Furthermore, our spirit colleagues say that we are no different after we die than we were while we were alive. *We are not miraculously changed at the moment of death.* We carry our thoughts, attitudes and desires with us in our astral bodies. To live in the city of God in a constant state of adoration of God is a goal that frankly most people would not enjoy. And frankly, most people—even when they die—are not ready for such an exalted goal. This does not mean that the possibility doesn't exist, it simply means that *most* people really don't want to spend their entire life adoring God—at the moment.

They have other interests they want to explore. And in a multi-dimensional universe, they have many lifetimes to explore and *satiate* those interests so that one day they may be pure enough to really want to appreciate and enjoy God. A problem is that on Earth, a life seems interminably long—while we're living it. Yet on the astral plane, there is no time. And to the people who live on the astral plane, a human life is only a short dream hardly remembered. Yes, this life that to you is so important and which takes up all your energy is only a flick of God's eyelash.

Most church doctrine holds there is only *one* life. Timestream indicates that's true. But the misconception is that it's one life on Earth. Rather, the life of a spirit is an eternal life composed of many, many experiences on many planets, in many dimensions, that help us to evolve into a higher state of being in which we become a fit being to live in God's presence. When the spirit at last moves into the celestial realms and returns to its source of energy, the life is completed. On the other hand, maybe it's really just beginning, only on a higher level!

If the universe is infinite, perhaps the soul is, too.

Buddha spoke of a multi-dimensional world that was a wheel—"the wheel of life." Man passed from the physical world to the astral plane, returning again to Earth to fulfill the desires he still had. If you wanted to "get off the wheel" you had to desire *nothing*. That is, when you wanted nothing else that Earth had to offer, you no longer returned to Earth. Your own desires are what pull you back to Earth. The obvious question to ask is: "What things do I still *want*?" For those are the things that hold you to Earth. A lot of free will is implied in reincarnation.

Many spiritual leaders believe that reincarnation occurs because of Karma—the Law of Action and Reaction. If you have hurt others, you have to return to Earth and suffer the same things you imposed on others. Hitler is an example. Many believe that Hitler will have to return to Earth to suffer what he did to others. We have another saying that applies: "What goes around comes around." Many of Christ's sayings can be looked at in terms of Karma: "Whatsoever you doeth to others, the same will be done to you." And his advice to always do good to others is wise in the Karmic sense. For if you only do good to others, then all you can receive in return is good. However, not every case of reincarnation is related to Karma.

The Technician says,

> It [reincarnation] is not always a process of reparation in this life for a past life. If people around you are hard hit by fate, do not always assume that they have to make up for past transgressions. Never judge! You may be wrong and are burdening yourself by your judgment. There are people whose grief and sickness were not imposed on them because of past Karma. They may have used their own free will to select a more difficult road to reach their goals [of increased wisdom and spiritual growth] faster.

The Technician goes on to say that "The human soul returns back to Earth often enough to learn all human life experiences..." before moving on to other dimensions. He describes it as a "constant evolution that moves forward," starting from the mineral state, moving from plants then to animals and then to human beings. He says there is no "backward evolution. The human soul does not return to Earth in the body of an animal."

Robert Monroe's research on the astral plane reveals that there are many such "consciousness growth centers or schools" like Earth in the universe. He comments that man is seeking "completeness" and that when a person has completed the Earth trip in its entirety (which includes many life-times), that soul is known for its love and wisdom.

Reincarnation, as our Timestream colleagues point out, is not something forced on spiritual beings. It is something a spiritual being willingly undertakes for his or her own knowledge, for wisdom. Many of our spirit colleagues did not believe in reincarnation when they lived on Earth. They discovered it to be a fact on the astral plane. Some of them do not want to return to the Earth at all, while others are now looking back to their return as a way of continuing their career or even of taking up a new endeavor.

For example, if there is a deep desire to learn music and be a performer that desire might draw one back to Earth. Still others are looking forward to moving on to a higher plane to learn wholly new possibilities and a wholly new way of living.

Spirit scientist Swejen Salter was asked by the Luxembourg experimenters how people on the third plane go about reincarnating. Isn't it hard to leave the families and friends they live with, and do these people decide by themselves how and when they incarnate?

Salter answered:

> In many cases, people decide themselves. In some cases they are also told by higher beings. Nobody is forced to return. To many, the process is like an inner voice that reminds them of their duties and

lessons that are still waiting for them on Earth. They may delay these tasks for many years, but know they cannot avoid them forever.

She goes on to say that some people meet with "more spiritually evolved beings," who tell them when it is time for the person to return to Earth. Still other people do not need a committee of guides, but they rely on their own inner voice that tells them what they need to finish on Earth. Whether they are counseled by a "Guide," a "Committee of Higher Spiritual Beings," or an "inner voice," the result is always the same. The person returns.

After the person has decided to reincarnate, he or she is led to a "special building" for the process of reincarnation. Salter describes the process:

> The procedure is similar to people's arrival here. Only this time it is a going back. The person is placed in what looks like a tub. His body, which on this level usually takes on an average age of 25-30 years, begins to change and becomes increasingly younger and smaller. It returns to the state of a child and then to a baby and finally to a small cell. By the time the body has become a cell, it is no longer present here among us. The cell has meanwhile arrived in the female body of a human being.

She says that in her world, the reincarnation process usually takes place "with the help of apparatuses." It is also possible to have the reincarnation process take place with the help of prayers and incantations. When the body has disappeared on the third plane, the conception has taken place and the "soul is in the cell." Still other research reveals that the soul may not necessarily have entered the cell, but that it remains close to the cell and may enter it anywhere between conception and birth. At any rate, the soul is in contact with the new mother and oversees the development going on in the cell.

The Luxembourg Lab asked Salter if any of the women at Timestream had had abortions during their Earth life. Salter replied:

> Yes, but it is not a topic of importance here anymore, such as on Earth. Here the emotions and feelings of guilt that arose on Earth about abortion are not playing a role anymore.

She went on to say that it's important to remember that we are eternal creatures, literally millions of years old, and that for an aborted fetus, generally, the period of being in the womb is only a short time. An abortion takes only a few minutes and is painful for only a moment.

To an aborted fetus, its memory of that painful time is as fleeting as a dark part of a dream. No one can extinguish the life of a soul. However, the mother may suffer great guilt from the act, which can torment her for a life-time. Yet, the decision for abortion differs in the case of each woman. Salter says:

> The women at Timestream who once said yes to an abortion did not make this decision out of lower motives. That is, they are free of the Karmic task of accounting for or repeating the experience. There is a great difference between the decision motivated by lower, selfish reasons and the one made out of desperation or in an emergency. Should a person (or a couple) decide on abortion only for reasons of convenience or to avoid a life task, higher spirit beings may decide otherwise [about their spiritual fate]. Although they will not be punished or judged, they will have to repeat and make up for what they avoided, possibly in a totally different form.

Incidentally, this is true of all life lessons. Master yogis have often said that the traditional penalty for abortion is that when a woman has aborted a child either in the present or a past life, she might not be able to have a child when she truly desires one. But as Timestream indicates, motive is important as to Karmic consequences. If a woman has the where-withal and security to have the child and her motive is to merely get out of responsibility, then the consequences are higher than if the woman is in desperate circumstances and is unable to properly raise the child.

The great guru Ramakrishna Ananda, who is still alive on Earth, points out that millions of souls are waiting to be born on Earth, to have the Earth experience necessary for their spiritual development and he often says to his devotees:

> Congratulations! You have a body! They're hard to get.

And that is why there may be karmic consequences. The woman who aborts a fetus interferes with the soul's spiritual progress. Considering there are millions of abortions on Earth, it's very hard indeed to get a body. And the waiting soul may have to wait what is equivalent to several lifetimes on Earth to finally get a suitable body which will enable the soul to have a life which will give it the particular experiences it needs.

Each soul is constantly evolving to a higher state. Yet spirit beings tell us that many people both in the physical world and the astral plane do not want to evolve. They prefer to stay where they are in their thoughts and attitudes. Some in organized religion believe that God will miraculously free them, so they wait apathetically for this liberation, forgetting that God has given them many precepts to work on and learn. However, our spirit colleagues tell us, "The soul must continue a long path of spiritual development which may lead through several reincarnations...." and, "We have to take our own steps toward progression." Yet, there is much help along the way, both here on Earth in the form of friends and counselors and in the higher planes, too, as angel Light Beings who try to counsel us spiritually.

Is there an end to reincarnation? The Technician says:

> When a man [or a woman] has experienced all facets of Earthly life, grief, joy, happiness, pain, suffering and exhaustion, when all search for knowledge was satisfied and he explored all corners of the Earth, when the wheel of life comes to a conclusion after many incarnations, then the time has come to look for new horizons.

The new horizons of which the Technician speaks is the next plane of existence, the fourth plane (or higher astral plane) and those above—planes which offer a more spiritualized expression of life. As the Technician says, "When man [or a woman] reaches the fourth plane...the person is freed from the law of reincarnation."

Just preliminary to reaching the fourth plane, men and women on the third plane come together in groups that have the same views and ideas, forming units that work and live together in harmony, peace, and accord.

But how many reincarnations are necessary to reach this lofty state of consciousness? The answer is, How much do you want to experience? You have galaxies to play in and to learn. For the adventurous, who love sensation, it might take millions. For the single pointed, spiritual person who wants to know God, the evolutionary path might be very short and quick. There is no set answer. It's up to you.

The great novelist Dostoyevsky once said something to the effect that there are two kinds of people in the world, those who go directly to God and those who go through Hell to find God. He added wryly that he was one of those people who had to go through Hell. Not that all lives of sensation are Hell, but a life of sensation is usually a combination of pleasure and pain.

The third (mid-astral) plane where many of the spirit scientists and their colleagues live is not a perfect plane. There is an evolution process occurring on the third plane which enables the people living there to move to higher dimensions or to return back to Earth. The final step on the third plane is to live in harmony and peace with others. Until this knowledge is learned, higher progression is not possible.

7

Heaven & Hell—

ANGELS, ADDICTS, MURDERERS, THE EARTHBOUND, AND SUICIDES

What most people consider heaven is located in the higher astral plane. Mystics and psychics call it "the Summerland."

In the Summerland, people live as we do and they look much as they did in their younger years. On this plane are the great colleges, design centers, beautiful landscapes with lovely plants and flowers, "paradise-like birds," animals such as cats and dogs, and animal species unknown on earth. There are many colors here that do not exist on earth and at first astral travelers are dazzled by them.

Dr. George Ritchie, physician and former President of the Richmond Academy of General Practice, had an experience on the astral plane in 1943. Ritchie was taken to a huge sphere-shaped building and he saw beings working on what he learned later was an atomic submarine. Nine years later, in *Life Magazine*, he saw a picture of the US's second atomic submarine—the same one he had witnessed being built years before on the astral plane.

Our spirit communicators tell us that many ideas are developed on the astral plane and then are given to inventors on earth. Often, when an inventor is intensely concentrating on a project, he is often working with an unseen partner who is in telepathic communication with him. Many inventors have said that they feel as if an unseen presence is beside them.

Many inventors have spoken about receiving valuable information in dreams, a favorite time for spirit scientists to communicate.

Tom Kubis, Pat Kubis' son, is an internationally known jazz composer. He played the piano at twelve without any lessons, and the first composition he played was George Gershwin's "Rhapsody in Blue"—an exceedingly difficult piece to play. He was composing in two weeks and was playing keyboard professionally within six weeks. In junior college, he received an award for Outstanding Pianist of 51 Colleges. He had never had a piano lesson. But he remarks, "When I first began to play, a man came into the room and sat beside me on the piano bench and he '*played through me*.' I learned everything from him." His spirit teacher loved a song called "Stella by Starlight," a song Tom had never heard before. It was only later, that a friend heard Tom playing it and told him the title.

Tom was told by several psychics that his mentor was Bach. Curiously, other psychics have reported that Bach is interested in modern jazz, which is what Tom writes. It may be that Tom's mentor is indeed Bach. Tom is forty-three now and still feels his mentor's presence.

I [Pat Kubis] was a college professor for twenty-three years at Orange Coast College in Costa Mesa, California; but I also taught at a campus on the astral plane. I often joked to friends who knew me well, "No wonder I'm so tired. I work all day on one campus and then on another on the astral plane." The curious thing is that the campus on the astral plane was just as "real" in every respect as the campus I taught at in Costa Mesa. However, the grounds and buildings of the campus on the astral plane were totally different and it was much larger than Orange Coast.

The main difference between Earth and the Summerland is that all of the people in the Summerland, people of all cultures, are living in peace and harmony. Indeed, this understanding of peace and harmony is a requisite for being able to move into the Fourth Plane, High Astral, which Indian mystics refer to as Devachan.

When a soul is ready to leave the astral planes and move to the mental-causal planes, there is a death of the astral body and a period of rest in which the soul reviews its progress. As previously stated, however, the soul may also decide to reincarnate as an option to learn more on the physical plane.

While the Third Plane has a strong resemblance to Earth, the Fourth Plane has less resemblance. Psychic researcher F.W. Myers, who died some years ago, has reported through mediums that the Fourth Plane is a world of consummate colors and forms. Beautiful lights and colors are experienced there. The soul has "the appearance of lights and colors quite unlike the human body...." The vibrations are much higher here and so the body is composed of much finer material.

The soul is not as isolated as it is on Earth or on the Third Plane; rather, it "becomes one with the other souls of its group." Only souls of the same vibration are visible to each other.

On this plane, the soul can use the power of "imagination" to appear visibly or invisibly either on Earth or on the mid-astral plane to help a friend or loved one. The soul is able to contact the dear one telepathically.

When a soul is ready to leave the Fourth Plane of colors and lights, again there is a death on this plane and a period of reviewing and assessing its spiritual progress. The soul has complete control over its form and outline. It may still decide to return to Earth for further knowledge. It selects according to its needs and experience whether to go on or come back.

Myers calls the Fifth Plane, the mental-causal plane, the Plane of Flames. Here, the soul appears as a flame. Meyers says that "there is a strong discipline, paired with limitless freedom, and strong feelings. Feverish activities and the passion and excitement of soul brothers flash through (the soul) like flames. Still, on this plane, one must struggle against despair, grief, and pain. But there is also ecstasy and joy."

The souls on this plane are aware of the feelings and unconscious life of plants, animals, and primitive souls, and one of their tasks is to "guide the destiny of new arrivals to the spirit world."

There is also a death on this plane, but no longer is there a "return to the limited human personality."

On the Sixth Plane, the Plane of Light, or celestial plane, the spirit is beyond all emotions. On this level, the soul is formless and appears as Light. Myers says: "Total equanimity of pure thought characterizes this level." The realities here are completely different from the worlds of matter and motion. Myers goes on to say that we do not have the words to adequately describe this realm.

Those souls who are strong enough to make the transition into "Timelessness" are now able to pass into the highest plane of all, the Seventh Plane, the Cosmic Plane of At-One-Ment. The soul at last fuses with the Source of Spirit. Though it merges with the Godhead, it still maintains its individuality. Now the soul is able to understand reality, the universe, and the soul lives in its spiritual design.

In this long spiritual odyssey of the soul, death is only a temporary resting place in which the soul can assess itself and its journey. At each death, the soul is surrounded by loving friends and relatives in spirit who encourage and console.

The Sixth and Seventh Planes are known as the celestial planes of God. Souls who remain on the sixth plane are able to "descend" with pure, constructive motives to "work in worlds of matter."

But why don't we on Earth see these celestial beings?

The Technician answers that humans rarely perceive them because most humans do not live a pure enough lifestyle to be aware of the celestial beings around them. While some humans do make efforts to "raise their consciousness," humans do not have the sensory equipment to see them, "hear their voices and see their signs."

If a human is able to surmount these challenges by various metaphysical practices, then another problem occurs. The actual experiences with the celestial being may conflict with various religious beliefs which have been handed down for centuries. Most of us have tried at one time the group experiment where one person whispers a sentence to another person who then repeats the sentence to the person next to them, and so on around the group. By the time the sentence has been received by the last person, the sentence has vastly changed. So religion has changed over the centuries, with many scriptures being edited and, knowlingly or unknowingly, changed by many translators. As ITC continues with its research, traditional religious beliefs will have to be altered, for today we are receiving direct transmissions from the astral planes.

Scientists and ITC experimenters are seeing first hand what life on the other side is like. No longer are there many varying conceptions about that other world. For while each man may have had his private conception of what an angel or his guardian angel might look like, we are now able to see the direct images of people who have made that transition into the next world, and we can get messages from those who are celestial beings.

Today, even the Beings of Light have transmitted pictures of themselves. Timestream scientists say of the Beings of Light:

> The difference between a higher spirit being and a human can best be visualized like this: a human is one personality; a higher being incorporates the attributes and knowledge of many human personalities in one being. Some of them are very close to the principle [God] the source and the center, and are far from the "existence of man."

Light Beings are angelic mentors. The Technician, who oversees Timestream, is an angelic mentor. He has never been human. The fourth plane is a plane of timeless truths or what Carl Gustav Jung called the archetypes. The Technician says that the closer one gets to the higher planes of life, the more healing power one has. Faith is like a beam of light that in time connects to the planes of light. Wisdom, knowledge, inspiration, protection and healing can be accessed across this bridge of light.

The Technician explains that faith is not blind hope, but rather a principle that is tangible, and the many healings at Lourdes and Fatima have occurred by *accessing the light.* At these locations, the faith of many people asking to be healed attracts "streams of bundled light energies" radiating from the higher planes.

On the fourth plane are the Akashic Records, the record of the lives of people who have lived on Earth and all the events that have ever occurred or will occur on Earth. The reflection of the Akashic Records can be seen on the third plane but it is not a true record as it is distorted due to the reflection.

This distortion has much to do with the wide range of psychics and their predictions. Most psychics are only able to access the third plane and the reflected Akashic Records. Consequently, their predictions are full of half truths. The spiritual psychic who is able to access the fourth plane is more accurate.

Beings of light communicate telepathically. The Technician says:

> When I talk to you I adopt certain characteristics of you, as I must "transfer" myself to you. Being other than human, a small part of myself has to adopt human characteristics [become human]. You would not understand me otherwise. The contacts are accomplished ...by your link-up....

And through that linkup, a portion of the Technician's energies are formed.

Salter adds that when the celestial beings speak among themselves, it is difficult for her to follow them with her mind. The mind of higher beings encompasses all languages of this world plus numerous languages of other worlds and their communication includes more letters, symbols and physical\technical formulae than any human can understand. Actually, she says, "the knowledge of higher beings can be received more accurately with the help of electronic equipment than with the mind of a single individual."

Another thing that makes communication difficult with celestial beings is that they have a non-human perspective and "human reactions are frequently alien to them."

When souls pass into the fourth plane, few of them are interested in contacting the Earth plane any more. The Technician says that beings on the fourth plane "have feelings, but they are no longer comparable with human feelings."

Salter mentions that "Mahatma Gandhi and Albert Schweitzer have gone beyond the fourth (higher astral) level and are now on the fifth (mental-causal) plane." They are no longer interested in physical beings and have "fulfilled their tasks toward mankind."

The Technician and Salter speak of the being *Pescator*, who is known on Earth as Jesus Christ. He is one of the few higher beings who has access to all the planes and still maintains contact with men on Earth. The Technician and Salter emphasize that Pescator is not an Earthly personality structure. He is capable of appearing in a human body, but He is not human and He is a differently structured personality.

Salter, the Director of Timestream, was assigned the project of developing the lab on the third plane by Pescator and she meets with Him, and six other higher beings, periodically to review the lab's progress. On one occasion, she took the physician Paracelus with her to the great conference room in the heavens where council meetings are held

> ...in a particularly beautiful room. The ceiling was a cupola in which numerous stars were shining brightly. Those stars were bigger and more luminous than the stars in your sky. The room turned on its axis.

Salter said the Technician asked her to present the suggestions of humans and report about ITC. It was difficult for her because of the higher beings' non-human perspective.

As she says, human reactions are frequently alien to them. Also, they hold back things from her, feeling that humans do not need to know everything because "the background of events and some information would be beyond their comprehension." Some events in life are "tied-up" with past lives and future experiences and a great deal of confusion might occur if humans had too much information.

She says that what is amazing about celestial beings is their sincerity. "They have no secrets from one another. They interact like a 'network' of computers, exchanging information as fast as a computer bank. If you speak to one of the higher beings, then all of the others are 'simultaneously' aware of the conversation. All of them are aware of your entire personality, too."

She goes on to say that, "As they have no secrets from each other, the only way one can get closer to them is by being absolutely sincere. Insincerity is alien to them. Nothing remains hidden in their dimension. You forget in your world that sincerity plays a most important part over here."

Salter says that higher beings take on the attitude of a grown-up towards a little child who cannot understand yet. Yet human beings today are not like little children anymore. They have evolved and expanded in knowledge.

Salter found that she had to learn to approach higher beings and convince them that she really, sincerely, wanted to communicate with them. And they, too, had to recognize that man's understanding had expanded enough that it was worth communicating with man.

When Paracelsus met the higher being Pescator, he said:

> He is a being of such pure light that it is almost blinding to look at him and of such divine beauty that tears rolled down my eyes.

Salter goes on to say of Pescator that He:

> ...has many personalities or aspects. The man on Earth called *Jesus Christ* is only one personality among others who belong to the entity *Pescator*.

Pescator told her that should Timestream be "faced with a decision to help the sick and needy or to totally concentrate on improving technical aspects of I.T.C., then [Timestream's] support and help for the needy should come first." So, although Timestream is a scientific endeavor, humanitarian concerns must take precedence over scientific concerns.

Salter explains that very little is known about the celestial planes, the planes of God, and that once one has reached these planes, one is never heard from again.

A Timestream contact coming over the radio describes the present life as just a fraction of a moment. He says, "The states of consciousness are very different here, but it is no reason to feel sad about it. A friendly world waits for all of us on the mid-astral and higher planes.

But if the higher planes offer a chance for friendship, loving companionship, a chance to grow and change, the lower planes hold man in a deadly noose of desire and negative behavior patterns. Dante's *Inferno* describes the various circles of hell: lust, greed, anger, hatred and malice. Even though he was writing in the medieval time, he was not inaccurate. If Hell is man's vices and addictions, human nature hasn't changed much.

The lower part of the astral plane, because of its "heavy" vibrations, is closest to the Earth. When a person dies, he or she goes to that part of the astral plane which is in accord with his or her emotional desires. The astral plane is created so that people with similar goals and similar emotional patterns are together. If a person is "preoccupied" with sex, there is a part of the lower plane where he or she can work out this negative desire. Not that sex is negative, but when the person is totally obsessed with sex, it becomes a vice.

Robert Monroe, who regularly travels the astral plane, describes many of the locales as "focuses" and once found himself on the sex plane. He says that he saw what looked to be a pile of maggots. On coming closer, he found hundreds of humans swarming over each other. He tried to pull one man out by the foot, but the fellow was so engrossed in sex, he stubbornly refused to talk to Monroe and burrowed more deeply into the pile.

Many alcoholics and cigarette smokers find themselves trapped on the lower plane as well. Their preoccupation leads them to hang around bars on Earth so they can vicariously pick up the effects of alcohol and cigarette fumes. They attach themselves to the auric field (an electro-magnetic field surrounding each person), like a parasite, trying to absorb into themselves the alcohol and nicotine. However, since they do not have a physical body, it becomes a hellish experience, like a thirsty man trying to drink water that is beyond his reach.

Many of these people free themselves of their unpleasant reality by undergoing rehabilitation processes on the mid-astral plane. The point is, that if we don't clean up our difficult habits and addictions on Earth, we'll have to do it later.

Some people become "Earth-bound" after they die. For example, a man or woman so preoccupied by a house he or she has built, will hang around it in spirit and the people living in that house might sense the spirit and will speak of "ghosts." Similarly, if the preoccupation is with a family member, for example a mother with a son, the mother will try to remain in contact with her son and not move up into the higher realms.

Dr. George Ritchie witnessed Earth-bound souls during his trip to the astral plane. In his book, *Return from Tomorrow*, he tells of an experience he had when he was twenty years old. He was pronounced dead of double-lobar pneumonia by an orderly and two doctors. Nine minutes later, he returned to life. During that time he saw Christ, who took him on a guided tour of the astral plane.

On the lowest part of the plane, which is closest to the earth, Ritchie described insubstantial beings standing in a bar on Earth, crowding around a drunken sailor, and greedily following each swallow he made. All at once, Ritchie saw a "bright cocoon" around the sailor open up and began peeling away from his head and shoulders. A moment later, one of the insubstantial beings jumped inside the sailor. Ritchie witnessed the same scene several times again with other men who were drinking. Each time, one of the insubstantial beings vanished into one of the men.

Ritchie realized that the insubstantial beings had developed an alcohol dependency that went beyond death. Now, even though they were dead, they hung around bars, hoping to take possession of anyone drinking so they could experience the effects of alcohol. As long as they craved alcohol, they were in a hell of craving.

Later, inside a house, he saw a boy in an insubstantial body standing in front of his mother and father, saying, "I'm sorry, Ma, I'm sorry Pa." But the man and woman could not hear him. Christ explained the boy was a suicide. Ritchie saw men who had murdered, now futilely boxing at each other—violent people who wanted to kill but could not because their intended victims were already dead. All of these were the earthbound, chained to earth by their addictions or vices, by hate and anger, chained to a world of which they were no longer a part. Now, these murderers were all together in a place where they kept trying to murder each other.

He had imagined Hell as a fiery place below the earth where men burned. Now he saw that they "burned" from their addictions and former destructive actions.

I [Pat Kubis] can confirm Ritchie's accounts. For many years in out-of-body trips, I traveled the astral plane, too.

On one occasion, I was shown the lowest part of the plane where murderers live. It was subhuman. The spirits there no longer looked like normal human beings. They were gross and deformed, and the atmosphere was very dense, almost black. I witnessed the liberation of one of these spirits.

He seemed to be incarcerated in a muddy substance with several other spirits. I asked the spirit, "What did you do?" It answered, "I killed. I was a murderer." This was said with much anguish. Then, a rescuer touched the spirit. The incarcerated spirit rose from the mud and the rescuer took its hand and they both left for a higher plane.

On another occasion I saw the sex plane. The locale was very dark and dim. It seemed to be a huge brothel with many, many cubicles where men and women engaged in sex on beds. Yet only a few feet away, I saw the rescuers waiting for those spirits who finally were freed from their preoccupation.

As George Ritchie saw, suicides roam the lower planes, too. There is no "escape" from life. You cannot escape your life or your problems by death. When you die, you still have a body, an astral body, and you still are confronted by your same problems and emotions.

The Technician says:

Avoiding work and responsibility in this world is only delaying the learning process. This is also true for those who are tempted to escape to a nicer world by taking their own life.

He says again and again that there is no escaping any personal problems. If you don't solve them now on Earth, they will be waiting for you on the next plane. Merely dying doesn't solve mental anguish and pain.

Another group of people trapped in the lower planes are those who have been killed in an accident and are traumatized, unable to leave the scene of the accident. Many psychics have reported the accident victim hovering over his or her lifeless body and trying futilely to talk to those people trying to help.

In all of these cases, the alcohol/cigarette/sex addicted, the murderers and the violent, the Earthbound, there are rescuers standing by, waiting, until the spirit has worked the attachment out of its consciousness. Then the rescuers are able to attract its attention and take the spirit to the higher realms of the astral plane. Many of the spirits on the third plane choose this task of rescuing spirits as their work.

Buddha advised people to "want nothing" as the path to the spirit's freedom; and Earth is the place to free the self from any harmful addiction. Milton's Satan said, "Where I am is Hell." ITC workers, Ritchie and Monroe, confirm Milton. We put ourselves in hell through allowing negative habit patterns to control us. But hell is not permanent. Only moments away— or sometimes years—waits a kind, compassionate soul, eager to help. No soul is in hopeless isolation on even the lowest of the astral planes.

The Technician says:

> The beyond [mid-astral planes] represents only one step of post-mortal existence. There are six other steps and the first one represents a huge nebulous region in which you wander about alone, should you have left the world by suicide or through other lowly motives. Those who believe in the theory of illusion, who claim mind and spirit totally dissolve when they leave your world, are wrong. Just the opposite. There are spirits who live in this nebulous world [the lower astral plane] between Earth and the beyond ....

The choice between heaven and hell is yours. Allowing any negative attitude or desire to take over condemns you to a lower plane in the astral world. There is no light and love there, only pain and anguish. *You will go to where you deserve to go.* Many people have heard these words from ministers and priests, but ITC confirms it. The "dead" are now able to communicate via telephone, TV and computer to tell us exactly what the next world is like. Your choice is important. It determines the next phase of your eternal existence.

No one knows exactly when he is going to die. Perhaps the Tibetan lamas offer the best advice on dying: Think only of God at that last moment. For when you die, your thoughts and feelings sentence you to the place you deserve on the astral plane.

8

Instrumental Transcommunication—

THE BEGINNINGS

In 1901, US ethnologist Waldemar Bogras traveled to Siberia to visit a shaman of the Tchouktchi tribe.[1] In a darkened room, he observed a spirit conjuring ritual. The shaman beat a drum more and more rapidly, putting himself in a trance state. Startled, Bogras heard strange voices filling the room. The voices seemed to come from all corners and spoke in English and Russian.

At first, Bogras wondered if the shaman was using ventriloquism. But how could he produce so many voices at once? Bogras decided to do a controlled experiment. He asked the shaman to come to his room where he could record the strange phenomena. After the session, Bogras wrote:

> I set up my equipment so I could record without light. The shaman sat in the furthest corner of the

[1]As reported by Eleanor Nogues in the French journal *Parasciences*.

room, approximately twenty feet away from me. When the light was extinguished the spirits appeared after some "hesitation" and, following the wishes of the shaman, spoke into the horn of the phonograph.

The recording showed a clear difference between the speech of the shaman, audible in the background, and the spirit voices which seemed to have been located directly at the mouth of the horn. All along, the shaman's ceaseless drum beats can be heard as if to prove that he remained in the same spot.

This experiment was the first in which voices of "conjured spirits" were recorded on an electrical recording device.

In the 1920's, Thomas Alva Edison, inventor of the electric light, motion picture camera and phonograph, was busily at work in his laboratory constructing a machine to achieve spirit communication with the dead. Edison told the *Scientific American*:

> If our personality survives, then it is strictly logical or scientific to assume that it retains memory, intellect, and other faculties and knowledge that we acquire on this Earth. Therefore, if personality exists after what we call death, it's reasonable to conclude that those who leave the Earth would like to communicate with those they have left here. I am inclined to believe that our personality hereafter will be able to affect matter. If this reasoning be correct, then, if we can evolve an instrument so delicate as to be affected, or moved, or manipulated by our personality as it survives in the next life, such an instrument, when made available, ought to record something.[1]

---

[1]*Scientific American* (October 30, 1920).

Edison's assistant, Dr. Miller Hutchinson, wrote:

> Edison and I are convinced that in the fields of psychic research will yet be discovered facts that will prove of greater significance to the thinking of the human race than all the inventions we have ever made in the field of electricity.

The mentalist Dunninger claims he saw the instrument Edison built and a GE engineer also claims to have worked on it. Unfortunately, Edison died before he could complete his invention.

Mrs. Edison told Norman Vincent Peale (author of *Power of Positive Thinking*) that when her husband died, he remarked to his physician: "It is very beautiful over there." Peale commented that Edison was a scientist, very factual, and as a scientist would never have reported "It is very beautiful over there," unless he believed it to be true.

Then, in the early 1950's in Italy, two Catholic priests, Father Ernetti and Father Gemelli, were collaborating on music research. Gemelli was President of the Papal Academy and Ernetti, an internationally respected scientist, physicist and philosopher, was also a music lover. They worked together in a physics lab with oscilloscopes, filter systems and other electronic gear in an effort to find ways to produce clearer singing voices.

For years, Father Gemelli had often silently called upon his deceased father for advice when he faced crisis situations. He'd never received a conscious reply from his father, but things seemed to work out; it was one of those reassuring rituals that everyone uses to get through tough times. Or so he thought.

On September 15, 1952, while Gemelli and Ernetti were recording a Gregorian chant, a wire on their magnetophone kept breaking. Exasperated, Father Gemelli looked up and asked his father for help. To the two men's amazement, his father's voice, recorded on the magnetophone, answered: "Of course I shall help you. I'm always with you."

The two men stared at each other shocked. Father Gemelli began to shake. Sweat broke out on his forehead. Was this the Devil? But Father Ernetti's scientific curiosity was piqued. He calmed Gemelli. "Come, come, let us try the experiment again." They did.

This time, a very clear voice filled with humor said: "But Zucchini, it is clear, don't you know it is I?"

Father Gemelli stared at the tape. No one knew the nickname his father had teased him with when he was a boy. He realized then that he was truly speaking with his father. Though his joy at his father's apparent survival was mixed with fear. Did he have any right to speak with the dead?

Eventually the two men visited Pope Pius XII in Rome. Father Gemelli, deeply troubled, told the Pope of the experience. To his surprise, the Pope patted his shoulder:

> Dear Father Gemelli, you really need not worry about this. The existence of this voice is strictly a scientific fact and has nothing whatsoever to do with spiritism. The recorder is totally objective. It receives and records only sound waves from wherever they come. This experiment may perhaps become the cornerstone for a building for scientific studies which will strengthen people's faith in a hereafter.[1]

---

[1] Italian journal *Astra* (June, 1990).

The good father was somewhat reassured. But he made certain that the experiment did not go public until the last years of his life. It wasn't until 1990 that the results were published.

In 1956, two California men, Attila von Szalay and Raymond Bayless, captured paranormal voices on audio tape. They reported their results in the Journal of the American Society for Psychical Research in the winter of 1959. The announcement was virtually ignored in the US; neither the Society nor the authors received a single response from readers.

In 1959, the man who was to become a great pioneer in the recording of voice phenomena, Swedish film producer Friedrich Juergenson, captured voices on tapes while taping bird songs. He was startled when he played the tape back and heard a male voice say something about "bird voices in the night." Listening more intently to his tapes, he heard another voice, that of his deceased mother say in German:

> Friedrich, you are being watched. Friedel, my little Friedel, can you hear me?

Juergenson said that when he heard his mother's voice, he was convinced he had made "an important discovery." During the next four years, Juergenson continued to tape hundreds of paranormal voices. He played the tapes at an international press conference and in 1964 published a book in Swedish: *Voices from the Universe* and then another entitled *Radio Contact with the Dead*.

He was a good friend of Pope Paul VI, having done a documentary film about him, and shared his research with him. The Vatican was so impressed, it authorized its own research people. Reverend Father Leo Schmid, a Swiss theologian, was given permission by his superiors to collect the voices and since 1969 has taped over ten thousand of them. Official authorization to conduct research into paranormal recordings was also given to Father Andreas Resch, who began a course in parapsychology at the Vatican's school for priests in Rome.

Father Pistone, Superior of the Society of St. Paul in England, stated in interviews and on TV that he didn't see anything dangerous in the voices. After all, the church has always held there is life after death. If the dead were able to contact us, then, it is a matter "which is under the power of God because the departed are under His power also." [1]

Pistone believes that, at the moment, the voices are a phenomenon and they need to be studied, and he indicated that the church would keep a close check on the research being done. Pope Pius' cousin, Dr. Gebhard Frei, co-founder of the Jung Institute and an internationally known parapsychologist stated that:

> Everything I have read and heard forces me to the supposition that only the hypothesis of the voices belonging to transcendental personalities has any chance of explaining the full scope of these phenomena.[2]

He added, "Whether it suits me or not, I have no right to doubt the reality of the voices."

In 1970, the International Society for Catholic Parapsychologists held a conference in Austria and a major part of that conference was concerned with papers on voice phenomena. In Ireland and England many TV shows discussed the tapes. Investigators

---

[1]*Handbook of Psi Discoveries*, p. 266-277.
[2]*Ibid.*, pp. 272-273.

examined the evidence and concluded the tapes were genuine and had not been tampered with. The publicity about the "voices" encouraged thousands of people all over the world to sit up at night with their tape recorders and to collect their own voices. The process was not complicated and many were successful.

Juergenson said that he had:

> ...found a sympathetic ear for the Voice Phenomenon in the Vatican. I have won many wonderful friends among the leading figures in the Holy City. [1]

Today "the communication bridge" stands firmly on its foundations. As Juergenson indicated, many churchmen saw or rather "experienced," the early audio research and were convinced it was genuine.

The Right Reverent Monsignor, Professor C. Pfleger comments: "Facts have made us realize that between death and resurrection, there is yet another realm of post-mortal existence. Christian theology has little to say about this realm."

His excellence, Archbishop H. E. Cardinale, Apostolic Nuncio to Belgium commented, "Naturally it is all very mysterious, but we know the voices are there for all to hear them."

Maurice Barbanell, editor of *Psychic News* remarked: "The future lies with instruments capable of recording vibrations or radiation emanating from the spirit world which are not normally receptive to man's five senses."

In 1967, Juergenson's *Radio Contact with the Dead* was translated into German, and Latvian psychologist

---

[1]*Ibid.*, p. 266.

Dr. Konstantin Raudive read it. Raudive was fascinated with the idea of contacting the dead, but he was skeptical. He decided to visit Juergenson to learn his methodology. Impressed, Raudive soon began developing his own experimental techniques. Like Juergenson, he, too, heard the voice of his own deceased mother, who called him by his boyhood name: "Kostulit, this is your mother."

Raudive conducted his experiments under strict laboratory conditions. He codified the principles and techniques relating to this new field, EVP (Electronic Voice Phenomena). It was Raudive who discovered that spirits needed white noise (a vibration) or carrier sound which they could modulate into voice patterns strong enough to be captured on tape. Now it was evident why Bogoras' shaman had used drum beats to provide the carrier sound!

Raudive found that the white noise between radio stations produced a rich spectrum of frequencies that spirit voices could manipulate into voices. His book, *Breakthrough: An Amazing Experiment in Electronic Communication with the Dead*, revealed his startling research.

However, scientists and electronic engineers remained skeptical of Raudive's work. Raudive's voices were different from human voices; they differed in pitch, amplification and intensity. The rhythm was irregular and had peculiar cadences. Raudive explained:

> The sentence construction obeys rules that differ radically from those of ordinary speech, and although the voices seem to speak the same way we do, the anatomy of their speech apparatus must be different from our own.

Only later, did a spirit communicator reveal that spirits have no larynxes. No one disputed that the voices were actually on the tapes. But at first, sound engineers believed that the tapes were picking up radio and television transmissions. Raudive knew this wasn't true, because many of the voices addressed him by name. And he had thousands of tapes.

In 1971, the chief engineers of Pye Records Ltd. decided to do a controlled experiment with Raudive. They invited him to their sound lab and installed special equipment to block out any radio and television signals. They would not allow Raudive to touch any of the equipment.

Raudive used one tape recorder which was monitored by a control tape recorder. All he could do was speak into a microphone. The engineers taped Raudive's voice for eighteen minutes and none of the experimenters heard any other sounds. But when they played back the tape, to their amazement, over two hundred voices were heard and twenty-seven of them were clear enough to be played back over a loud speaker. The control monitor's tape was blank. What had happened was theoretically impossible!

Two observers, publisher Sir Robert Mayer and his wife, Lady Mayer, received messages from a deceased friend, Arthur Schnabel, who spoke in German to them. Other voices directly addressed Raudive as "Kosti" or "Koste," and Raudive's deceased sister said her name three times: "Tekle."

Sir Robert was so elated by the experiment he agreed to publish a book on the subject. He jokingly remarked that he was "relieved at the thought that eternity does not mean being condemned to eternal inactivity." Perhaps the most powerful communication Raudive received, out of almost 100,000 recordings, was a Latvian voice that said: "There is no death here. The Earth is death."

Also in 1971, the English company Belling and Lee, Ltd., decided to conduct some experiments with Raudive at their Radio-Frequency-Screened Laboratory. Some scientists had theorized that perhaps the voices were coming from ham-radio broadcasts and bouncing off the ionosphere. The supervising engineer, Peter Hale, was a physicist and an electronics engineer. Hale was considered the leading expert on electronic-suppression in Great Britain, and one of the five leading sound engineers in the West. Belling and Lee is used by the British government to test its most sophisticated defense equipment. What happened baffled the sound engineers. Again, paranormal voices were recorded on factory fresh tape. Hale said, "In view of the tests carried out in a screened laboratory at my firm, I cannot explain what happened in normal physical terms."

In 1969, Dr. Raudive shared a First Prize award from the Swiss Association for Parapsychology along with Swiss physicist Professor Alexander Schneider for their discoveries of direct voice messages on tape.

Many of Raudive's friends and colleagues, inspired by his work, began experiments in this new field of EVP. Swiss physicist Alex Schneider discovered that many of the spirit voices could not be heard by the human ear during recording, but they could be heard while playing back the tape. High frequency engineer Theodor Rudolf, an employee of the German communications company Telefunken, developed the "goniometer" and electronics engineer Franz Seidl developed the "psychophon," both sophisticated recording devices.

Because of the great pioneering experiments made by Raudive, many experimenters today refer to the short, faint voices of EVP as "Raudive voices."

Scottish researcher, Alexander Macrae, studied hundreds of the Raudive voices and found that they lasted an average of 1.8 seconds. All of the experimenters worked toward getting longer, stronger voices in dialogue that would help turn their invisible friends into allies that could convey useful information to Earth. If only there were a way to transmit pictures from the spirit realm to Earth!

In 1969, German experimenter, Hanna Buschbeck, founded the German "Electronic Voice Association" and published a newsletter to report the results which European experimenters were achieving.

Then, in the 1970's, a significant breakthrough occurred. Ironically, it occurred in the US where EVP had been virtually ignored. Retired industrialist George Meek and his wife Jeannette had been traveling around the world with teams of researchers to explore first hand spiritual healing, materialization, and other paranormal phenomena. In 1973, the Meeks met a psychically gifted man, William (Bill) O'Neil, who had been having some fascinating and rather bizarre materialization experiences at his Pennsylvania home.

One evening, Bill's wife Mary Alice, also psychically gifted, went into a trance. Suddenly, a young girl materialized in their living room. She said her name was Lorna and she was looking for her mother. But as soon as Mary Alice came out of her trance state, the child vanished.

Meanwhile, Bill was having some very interesting psychic experiences of his own. In his upstairs lab, he had a spirit visitor named Doc Nick, a deceased ham radio operator. Bill could see him clearly and he tried to tape Doc Nick's voice.

But when he recorded his conversations with Doc Nick, only his own voice was captured on tape. Naturally, it worried him since he could not prove whether the voice of Doc Nick, that he heard in his head, was real or a delusion. Also, only he could see Doc Nick. His wife couldn't. Bill tried to take pictures of Doc Nick, but the photos were blank.

Frustrated, Bill became exasperated with his failures to record any evidence of Doc Nick and he lit a fire, intending to burn the blank pictures. Just as he was about to toss the first photo into the fireplace, he felt a hand on his shoulder. Thinking it was Mary Alice, he turned.

Startled, he saw a tall, well dressed gentleman. Fearfully, Bill realized that it was another spirit materialization. The spirit said he needed Bill's help on a research project involving improved EVP communication. In a black mood, Bill replied, "No one will believe it anyway, so what's the use?"

The spirit assured Bill he'd give him plenty of documentation. "On Earth I was Dr. George Jeffries Mueller. I was a university professor and a NASA scientist." He smiled. "I can give you my social security number, my family and career history, and even some unlisted phone numbers of former colleagues, if you want them?"

Skeptical, Bill shrugged. "Who will believe me?"

At that moment, Mary Alice spoke up from the doorway. "I'll believe you, Honey. I see him, too."

Bill jerked around. "Can you hear him speaking?"

"I can see his lips moving, but I can't hear him," she replied.

That was the beginning of an astonishing collaboration between dimensions: Doc Mueller and Doc Nick in spirit, helping Bill O'Neil on Earth design a new piece of electromagnetic equipment that would convert spirit voices into audible voices.

The project almost didn't get off the ground, however, because the O'Neils were broke and the many paranormal events in their home had left Bill shaken and unstable emotionally. He had serious doubts about continuing paranormal investigation. However, George Meek, who had been helping the O'Neils out for four years, giving Bill an occasional check to continue his paranormal experiments, felt that Bill was really on to something.

"Look," he said, "I'll give you sixty dollars a week to keep working on the communication project with Doc Mueller and Doc Nick." Bill did not like taking handouts, but considered the money as pay for a job that only he could do. He continued with the work.

Ironically, in the next few months there developed a competitive rivalry between Doc Mueller and Doc Nick as they helped develop a spirit communication machine, "Spiricom." The machine produced a set of tones and frequencies that spanned the range of the adult male voice. The rivalry puzzled Bill, for he'd assumed that once people made their transition to spirit, petty human emotions would disappear.

George Meek, who'd been doing experiments on his own for many years, assured Bill that such feelings were normal for beings operating at a "low level" of spirit—that is, at spiritual frequencies which exist near the physical world. George said that in order for Doc Nick and Doc Mueller to communicate with Bill, they needed to "descend," or "lower their frequency" to be near the Earth; and in so doing, they resumed many of their Earthly thought patterns, emotions and behaviors.

Finally, on October 27, 1977, after several months of experimenting, the voice of Doc Nick came through on Spiricom. His voice could barely be heard through the heavy tones of the equipment, but after all the effort that had gone into the project, even this was a remarkable accomplishment. That history-making dialogue began:

> **Bill:** Try it again.
>
> **Doc Nick:** All right. Do you hear me now, Bill? Can you hear me, Bill?
>
> **Bill:** Yeah, but you make it sound just like...Oh boy...a robot on television.
>
> **Doc Nick:** Yes, we always will, when we ...we will. The one thing ...you hear, Bill. You hear, Bill?
>
> **Bill:** (Nervously adjusting the frequencies): Yeah, okay. You have to forgive me but...I know this is... you have to admit this is kind of scary.
>
> **Doc Nick:** Why are you...leave it alone, leave it alone. Did you hear me, Bill? Do you hear what I say?
>
> **Bill:** Yeah, I got it now, Doc....

In the ensuing years, Doc Mueller gradually moved into the research picture as Doc Nick moved out.

By the fall of 1980, with the help of Doc Mueller (who had studied electronics during his life-time), Spiricom had advanced to the point where the spirit voice, although quite buzzy, was easily understandable.

On Easter Sunday in 1982, George Meek held a press conference at the National Press Club in Washington DC. to announce the success of Spiricom—the Meek-O'Neil project had made contact with the mind of a NASA scientist who had died fourteen years earlier. Not only had they made contact with Dr. George Jeffries Mueller, but they had gone on to hold over twenty hours of extended dialogue with the man or rather, with the dead man's mind, memory, personality and soul—what we generally refer to as the spirit.

The pioneering work of George Meek and Bill O'Neil in inter-dimensional communication planted seeds and fueled minds all around the world. Sarah Estep started the American Association of Electronic Voice Phenomenon (AA EVP) in 1982 and quickly assembled a list of hundreds of EVP experimenters to receive her newsletter.

In Europe, thousands of people were already following up on the EVP experiments of people like Friedrich Juergenson and Konstantin Raudive. Meanwhile, George, Bill, and their spirit colleagues had carried EVP a step further. Rather than getting short, faint voices on tape, the Spiricom system allowed, for the first time in history, extended instrumental dialogue with the spiritual world.

Spiricom launched in the new field of ITC, or Instrumental Transcommunication—the use of electronic systems to undertake meaningful communication across dimensions. Thus, George Meek and Bill O'Neil are usually regarded as the fathers of ITC, just as the Wright Brothers are regarded as the fathers of modern flight.

And just as airplanes got bigger and better as younger minds built upon the foundation, so has ITC flourished since Spiricom.

In 1986, German experimenter Klaus Schreiber received instructions on his tape recorder to turn on the TV. The result was a picture of his deceased daughter Karin. Soon, he was receiving more paranormal images including one of Albert Einstein.

Most notable among the new generation of ITC researchers are Maggy and Jules Harsch-Fischbach of Luxembourg, Directors of CETL, the Sound Lab in Luxembourg whose work won the 1992 Swiss Award for Paranormal Discoveries and is detailed in this book.

Amazingly, Friedrich Juergenson and Dr. Konstantin Raudive, the great pioneers of EVP, along with Klaus Schreiber mentioned above, have died and are now coming across on television, computer, radio, telephone and fax. On June 12, 1992, Friedrich Juergenson told the eagerly watching ITC experimenters on Earth:

> Every being is a unity of spirit and body that cannot be separated on Earth or in spirit. The only difference is the fact that the physical body disintegrates and in its place comes the astral body.
>
> Some theologians among us consider the possibility that the astral body resolves in absolute spirit now and then. When you leave your area of time and space, your consciousness remains the same. What happens afterwards cannot be explained properly with words anymore. This is perhaps the reason why so many theories develop among you, some of which are mediumistic.
>
> Our message is to tell you that your life goes on. Any speculations on how an individual will

experience it are bound to be limited in validity. All your scientific, medical or biological speculations miss the mark of these realities. What serves as "real" to science is not close to reality in the broad picture. It is no more than a word in a book.

On November 12, 1992, Dr. Konstantin Raudive said this to Luxembourg experimenter Maggy Harsch-Fischbach:

None of you has to die to be the person you would really like to be. You have only to die because you selected one of many possibilities for yourself. The person who has become panicky and fears death may wish to recall that he has selected his death long before in another dimension.

We cannot explain these psychological processes and the variety of possibilities within the limits of ITC contacts. You can, however, learn from us through your mediumistic and intuitive faculties which you all have but only a few of you use creatively.

Today, Konstantin Raudive and Friedrich Juergenson add a new dimension to their roles as paranormal experimenters. From their perspective on the astral plane, they have become philosophic mentors as well, for a different dimension has new paradigms and a new philosophy must necessarily and inevitably emerge.

9

Purpose of Timestream Lab & CETL (Luxembourg Lab)

Many people have asked, "Why is Timestream contacting us now?" The "dead" have long been trying to contact us and they have achieved some modest success during the past hundred years, through mediums and psychics. Now we are in an age of high tech and at last we have instruments through which they can make a direct transmission without having to come through the mind of a human being. Trying to communicate through a medium's mind is rarely accurate, because the medium is translating what he or she receives and the human mind often "colors" the information.

The primary message is "We are not dead. We are alive. There is life beyond the grave." And now, there is the equipment necessary to establish scientific knowledge of the continuity of life, providing apparent proofs. The mission of Timestream is just beginning, and it may take many years to establish enough proofs so that all of mankind can accept the idea that immortality is a fact, a law of the universe. The work that is to be accomplished is nothing short of changing modern man's whole way of thinking about life itself. As said before, philosophy and religion, too, will have to change to accept this new paradigm of being.

Another goal of Timestream is to open a permanent link between the Earth and the astral plane. Through this link, this "bridge," some of the greatest minds of all time, such as Edison, Madame Curie, Nikola Tesla, and other great scientists, may continue to share their knowledge with us to help heal our planet of pollution and societal problems.

The third plane already has powered cars and other more highly developed modes of transportation. Their engineers and ours may one day collaborate on new inventions that will solve pollution problems.

Deceased physicians at Timestream hope to medically assist mankind: "spirit doctors" helping medical doctors to heal. Spirit doctors have long helped doctors on Earth through telepathy, giving telepathic instructions. Many surgeons have said that while they are operating, it is as if "somebody is working through them, using their hands." This is true. Spirit doctors are there in the operating room, trying to help. Many doctors say they pray and meditate to receive input from a higher source.

It may well be that in times to come, a doctor on Earth will be able to tune a television set to a certain frequency to discuss a case with "a committee" of deceased doctors who are specialists in his field.

Another of Timestream's goals is to help man understand the role of animals on Earth and also to help animals. Timestream is against animal experimentation. Animals are living creatures with a destiny. They are evolving into a higher life form and how they are treated now, on Earth, will influence them as a higher life form. If an animal is treated kindly and with love, that animal will be a loving being. But if an animal is treated cruelly that animal can be a cruel, heartless being with thoughts of revenge and hatred that will inevitably play out in some later life.

Dr. Konrad Lorenz, deceased now, but alive on the third plane, is in charge of the animals who arrive on the astral plane in the community of Timestream. Swejen Salter says that he searches with his monitors for locations where animals have died violently and he uses technical processes to bring those animals into the spirit dimension. The animals find themselves alive again in familiar surroundings, but this time there is no war or environmental pollution. Salter says that this method is also used to locate human beings who died violently and are still wandering aimlessly around their bodies.

Lorenz was particularly upset about the innocent animal victims of the Gulf War who were badly mutilated by gunfire and bombs. He said, "It made me ashamed that I was once a human being."

Lorenz, a professor on Earth, did not believe in life after death, but he found himself very much alive after he died. He consented to participate in ITC activities because he could help people come to new understandings of the cosmos. To him, the fact that his life continued was not as important as the enlightenment he might bring to other people.

Another area of interest to Timestream is to reveal to mankind that there are consequences to crime. Nobody really "gets away" with anything. Timestream confirms the ancient teachings that there is a band of energy or consciousness which surrounds our planet, the "Akashic Records." Inscribed on the Akashic Records is every event that ever happened on Earth and, most psychics say, every event that *will* happen. Although, they also say that many of these events can be changed. For example, Edgar Cayce read the Akashic Records and saw a huge shifting of the earth before the year 2000. But he felt that man could change that catastrophe if he changed his attitude and his whole life style. However, if man continued on his present course, those events would surely happen.

The Akashic Records can be accessed by those on the higher planes and also by gifted psychics on Earth. The entire scene of a crime can be observed. However, high tech adds another dimension to the Akashic Records. In a future scenario, in the case of a murder, the victim—now alive in the third plane— will be able to give testimony against his or her murderer. Obviously, judicial law as we know it will be changed.

Philosophy and religion, too, will have to be modified. So many religious teachings are ego oriented ideas of the leaders who founded those religions. Many of these ideas are divisive and cause dissension and wars. Timestream hopes to foster cooperation and understanding among all the religions of the world.

CETL, the main receiving lab on Earth, is primarily a research facility and the experimenters there are committed to opening the lines of communication between Earth and the astral plane. CETL considers itself as an observation post, recording the information received. CETL's directors, Maggy and Jules Harsch-Fishbach, want to encourage research scientists to work in the field of Transcommunication and they hope to encourage research groups around the world. They want to encourage unity among scientists and research groups that study and work in the field of Transcommunication.

One overriding message that CETL hopes to convey is that *"We Are All One."* Our souls, our spirits, are not to be separated from each other. Higher souls do not see us as separate individuals. As long as we on Earth see ourselves as separate from the whole, we will live in separation, isolation and sorrow.

People on the third plane come from all periods of time, from many different cultures, and yet they all live in peace and harmony together. The electronic bridge which the astral plane has built to our planet is to help us free ourselves from racism, patriotism and nationalism so that we may achieve an international unity and cooperation on Earth. We are fortunate to live in a time when most of us will see in a very concrete way that another dimension exists and that the people there are holding out their hand to us.

10

Getting Started—

THE EQUIPMENT YOU NEED TO DO YOUR OWN RESEARCH IN INSTRUMENTAL TRANSCOMMUNICATION (ITC)

If starting out in ITC could be summed up in a single word, the word would be *caution*. In order for spirit beings to contact us through our systems— whether manifesting their faint EVP voices on audiotape or showing up on photographic film, the beings themselves need to get close to the physical plane in terms of their vibratory rate. That is, they need to be in the lower levels of the spirit worlds where substance is denser and more Earth-like than what we would find in the higher worlds.

In these lower worlds there is less love and more fear than in the higher worlds. There is less compassion and more malevolence. In other words, the beings there are more "human," less Godly, and so all sorts of personalities can be accessed by the aspiring ITC experimenter who proceeds without the proper precautions and protection.

ITC, as it exists today, is something quite new and unusual for the spiritual dimensions associated with Earth. It involves the plans and coordination of very high spiritual beings working with other spiritual beings on many levels. The messages and images which these beings send to Earth must be channeled through a sending station such as Timestream which exists near the Earth, in the lower spirit worlds.

Not only the Earth experimenters, but also the sending station and the spirit colleagues who serve there, all need to be kept under an umbrella of protection that is maintained by higher beings and guardian angels. Everyone in ITC must maximize love and minimize fear in all aspects of their lives in order to remain free of negative, unpleasant energies.

So, people wishing to get involved in ITC can find the needed protection in three ways—prayer, positive thinking and a good rapport with colleagues based on love and unity of thought. *Praying* with passion from the heart can bring us everything we need in life, including spiritual protection. *Positive thinking* involves getting in the habit of pushing negative thoughts out of our mind as they come up and replacing them with positive thoughts. Negative thoughts are those that are related to our fears, frustrations, resentments and hatreds. When we are consumed by negative thoughts we draw lower, negative beings into our life, and higher beings avoid us as we might avoid someone, say, with terribly bad breath. Positive thoughts are the product of our love, trust and appreciation, and these aspects of ourselves draw higher beings into our life. Lower beings keep away from positive thinkers like scavengers keep away from live, healthy animals or people.

Establishing a rapport with colleagues and friends based on love and unity of thought is probably the most powerful protection for anyone involved in spiritual work.

GETTING STARTED

When getting started in just about anything there are certain basics to consider. In ITC those basics include the three means of protection just listed. They also include efforts to get voices on audiotape. These short, faint EVP voices are usually the first instrumental contacts a person will get. Following are some suggested steps for getting started in EVP and, later, ITC work.

GET THE BASICS

Acquire one or two audiocassette *recorders*—one to be used to record paranormal voices, the other (optional) one to generate a source of noise which the spirit beings will modulate to create EVP voices. In addition to the tape recorder(s), you will need one *microphone* with a built-in preamplifier and perhaps an audio *mixer* (to amplify the microphone) and a set of *headphones* for concentrated listening.

As you might imagine, much of this work involves frequent playback of short excerpts of the recorded tape in order to listen closely for paranormal voices. Therefore, the best tape recorders for EVP experiments have a fine speed control and a REVIEW key which quickly rewinds the tape to the last starting point without having to push STOP-REWIND-STOP-PLAY.

It is best to use a separate microphone, even if the cassette recorder has a built-in mike, and it is best to have this external mike plugged into a mixer to control its volume while recording.

After feeding the microphone into the mixer and the mixer into the recorder, position the microphone about five feet from the recorder. Turn the volume down low while you ask questions. Turn the volume up while you wait quietly for answers. Here is an example of what your part of the dialogue might be:

Today is April 15, 1995. It is 9:30 p.m. (pause)

I would like to establish contact with those on the other side. (pause)

Good evening, dear friends, this is (name/names). I/we greet you. (pause)

I would like to thank you for yesterday's answers. (pause)

Today I would like to speak with (name/names). (Pause)

Dear (first name/names), I hope you are present this evening and can hear me. (pause)

My first question ...

EVP experiments can be conducted in a quiet area or with a background noise source. They can be conducted alone or with a group. There are several considerations for each option:

By experimenting in a quiet space, the EVP voices stand out clearly on tape, but often the spiritual being lacks the energy to make his messages loud enough to be noticed or long enough to be meaningful.

A noise source acts as "fuel" for the spiritual being's voice capability. He can modulate the sound energy in order to plant louder, longer messages on tape. When you play back the tape, however, it is sometimes difficult to distinguish the voice from the background noise. As a noise source, canned "white" noise or a taped radio program provides a rich range of frequencies from which the spirit being can work. Taped songs or noise of any sort can also work.

By experimenting alone you eliminate the problem of other people's "bad vibes" harming the contact, but, unless you are a powerful telepath, you face the problem of working with a weak energy field, or "contact field."

Experimenting in groups often requires considerable effort to nurture unity and harmony in the group in order to develop the needed contact field, but once you succeed, that field is a strong one.

CONTACT FIELD

Developing a strong, healthy contact field with spiritual beings "near" to you—deceased loved ones, deceased people whom you have always deeply admired—is the most important aspect of ITC. (*Strong* here implies developing your psychic skills; *healthy* implies developing your spiritual nature.)

When there develops an awareness between two beings, be they human or spiritual, a field of life energy is generated. This life energy goes by such names as subtle energy, chi, Qi, shakti, orgone energy, kundalini and Holy Spirit. While developing an awareness for a spiritual being comes more naturally to people with psychic or clairvoyant skills, anyone can do it. Whenever we concentrate on a friend out of the past, we develop a *contact field* with that person. When we concentrate on a deceased loved one, we develop a contact field with the spirit of that person. As we practice this art of concentration, the contact fields we create become stronger and the influence we exert on the other beings becomes greater. Some people call this developing our psychic or telepathic skills.

In the dense physical world, the contact field of the average person is scarcely noticeable to anyone but the most sensitive telepaths. In the subtle worlds of spirit, the contact field is more noticeable. Passion builds a strong field. A husband grieving for a deceased wife can actually pull her spirit to his side with his intense yearning.

Lusting after a neighbor's spouse creates an *unhealthy* contact field, because we are destabilizing *our* family, *their* family, and to some degree the entire neighborhood. Sending heartfelt love toward a neighbor's family creates a *healthy* contact field as it adds strength and stability to the social groups around us all.

In a similar vein, when we go about developing a contact field with spiritual beings, we should *always* act out of love, *never* out of fear, anger or other negative emotions. Our loving feelings will draw loving spirit beings to us, bringing us profound happiness. Our base or vile feelings will invariably draw base and vile beings to us who can literally ruin our lives. With patience, persistence and a good attitude, we eventually will begin getting messages from spirits of loved ones.

ADVANCING FROM EVP TO ITC WORK

It would be nice to be able to study the ITC successes occurring today in various countries, configure similar systems in our homes and start getting the same astonishing results. Unfortunately, it doesn't work that way. Building and strengthening a healthy contact field over a period of time seems to attract capable help from the higher levels of spirit, and without that help it is apparently impossible at this time for us on Earth to make the advanced ITC connection.

With continued dedication and enthusiasm we may eventually make contact with a higher being who will direct us toward advanced ITC work. If this occurs, we can expect to move ahead quite rapidly. So as we pray for help, especially advice for improving our communications, our prayers are answered.

The higher spiritual beings—angels, Beings of Light, ascended Masters, etc.—are eager to see Earth become more like the Heavens. This is told to us by all the time-proven religions, and it is being told to modern ITC researchers as well, by their spiritside collaborators.

When we begin contacting the other side—make no mistake about it, they have their eye on us—and if our efforts are earnest and our motives are based on love, we will probably get assistance.

TIPS FOR BEGINNERS

At first it is best to ask only two or three questions, as it takes about an hour of listening for each five minutes of recording.

It is best to try to contact deceased loved ones and friends at first, because with your love you already have established a contact field with these people, and also because you know intimate details of their lives and can therefore assess the validity of the contact and the messages.

Ask questions that solicit longer answers, rather than, "How are you?"

Keep in mind that spirit beings can read our thoughts and feelings, and that their voices are not usually audible while they are being placed on tape.

Also keep in mind that people with strong telepathic skills, whether innate or developed, can generate strong contact fields. If you or someone in your experimenting group has these skills, your chances for early success are better. If your telepathic skills are not strong, you will still get results but it may take longer.

Negative feelings—fear, anger or resentment—can draw troubled spiritual beings to you and your group indiscriminately, and the messages you will receive could be unnerving, or even worse, your lives could be badly disrupted. Better to experiment when you are happy and at peace, and to ensure that everyone in your group is a happy, loving person. If someone in the group has had a bad day, raise their spirits. *Always* foster harmony and unity in the group.

The safest and most successful experimenters are fully aware that *every one has a spirit protector, or guardian angel*, and they always pray to that higher being for assistance before each session. In fact, it is wise for each of us to nurture daily our relationship with our own personal angel.

The best contacts are usually made in the wee hours of the morning—say two to four a.m. Since it is neither fun nor "normal" for most of us to be up at that time, the next best time to make contact is late evening, before bed.

Apparently it takes considerable effort and energy for our spiritside colleagues to give us EVP messages, so quite often the only message received is the name of the experimenter or the name of the being.

EVP voices rush by quickly and have an unusual timbre. They are often grammatically incorrect. The last syllable of a word may rise, giving the voice a sing-song quality. Sometimes the last syllables are dropped altogether as though energy has run out, making the message sound staccato.

The other side seems to want researchers whose curiosity drives them to experiment. They shy away from individuals who want to be successful at any cost in order to dazzle large audiences. Higher beings are also pulled to help people praying with passion for help, or longing for a loved one. They are drawn strongly to help spirit children.

Experiment in small steps. Don't fear criticism. Don't let others stand in your way of seeking the truth you desire. Contribute to society. Become a spiritual philosopher.

Finally, the seriousness of communicating with the worlds of spirit cannot be overemphasized. Weekend hobbyists and dabblers are likely to get themselves into trouble. Also, the problems they create become fuel for those who fight against *all* inter-dimensional communication, usually out of fear and religious dogma.

11

The Latest Spirit Contacts in Luxembourg—

A MESSAGE FOR JULIET; A DOG NAMED TERRY; AND JULES VERNE.

Back in the 1950's, Juliet Hollister of Connecticut dreamed of a better world. She began a project that, unknown to her at that time, would last a lifetime, taking her around the globe to meet spiritual leaders and religious dignitaries of many faiths. With the help of Eleanor Roosevelt, Juliet founded the Temple of Understanding, which today is a United Nations NGO (nongovernmental organization) that is sometimes called "the Spiritual UN." Its role is to help increase understanding and compatibility among the world's religions.

Eleanor Roosevelt, of course, played a key role in getting the United Nations on its feet with the intent that this new international body would provide the best leadership the world ever had. Considering the struggling, warring, fragmented state of the world *before* the formation of the UN, the UN has done much to fulfill Mrs. Roosevelt's dreams—though much is still left to be done.

After I [Mark Macy] got to know Juliet Hollister in 1993, it occurred to me that if she met Maggy and Jules Harsch-Fischbach in Luxembourg, only good things would come of it. Juliet, too, had a strong desire to meet the Harsch-Fischbachs. In January of 1994 I sent a letter to suggest the meeting. Within a week of receiving my letter, Maggy received a fax from her spirit friend and mentor Swejen Salter at Timestream:

> You know that Pescator has many personalities, or aspects. The man called on earth Jesus Christ is only one personality among others who belong to the entity Pescator.
>
> In fact, one of these personalities is someone you would call an intercessor for the older woman Mark reported about. The union between them is due to the fact that Mrs. Hollister is working for the "Temple of Understanding."
>
> You know that Eleanor Roosevelt, who helped her to create it, is trying together with Bill O'Neil to build a contact bridge from our world to yours.
>
> But Mark is well informed. I don't have to tell you more.
>
> For the evolution of ITC, it would be important to meet the lady one day, perhaps during summer in Luxembourg.

Juliet Hollister and her niece Alison van Dyk, both of whom have done much to help ITC in the US, received an invitation to visit CETL and they invited me [Mark] along to introduce them to Jules and Maggy.

Maggy and Jules picked us up at the hotel at eleven a.m. and we went to their home, observing historic sites and points of interest in the charming city of Luxembourg along the way.

We sat around the dining room table, drank sparkling water and got to know each other much better. According to Maggy, that casual conversation played a crucial part in establishing the needed energy or bridge for a contact with Timestream that day. It helped bring our vibrations into harmony.

As we sat around the table talking about ITC and ourselves, Maggy eventually rose and walked over to the GA-2 configuration, which the couple had set up in their living area in front of the TV. It included a portable stereo radio with two detachable speakers, a small battery-operated radio with a dish antenna, two extra speakers with built-in power supplies, and a tape deck with a microphone to record the contact.

The two radios were tuned to different frequencies between stations so that there was a low hissing of white noise. It wasn't long before a high-pitched voice could be heard very weakly: "Contact."

It was the voice of Technician.

Maggy immediately replied, "Hello? Hello?" She adjusted the dials for a moment, then stepped aside as we all listened intently. In about fifteen seconds, the white noise of the radios began to fade away and the deep, familiar voice of Konstantin Raudive became louder and louder.

Following is an edited transcript of the English part of the contact, minus some highly personal information for Juliet Hollister.

1994 July 30, 12:34

TECHNICIAN: Contact.

K. RAUDIVE: It can only work when the vibrations of those present are in complete harmony and when their aims and intentions are pure.

Juliet Hollister, you have many friends not only on your side but also on this side of the veil. Now that you have come to the autumn of your life and when you can look back on the situations you lived and all the work you did, some of your actions seem to you far away and nearly vanished in the dawn. But others subsist splendidly and in full light.

You still will be given many years to complete and round up the project you undertook. And it is only then that you will come home, returning to those who were with you once and who are dear to your heart.

Dear Alison van Dyk, we know that life has not been easy for you on many occasions, but be reassured that your passing here at this contact bridge will mark a turning point in your existence. Especially the children on Earth owe you very much. The children are the future of the world. You, Alison, are one of the builders of this new, better world.

Finally, last but not least, Mark Macy. My dear friend, we bring our greetings to colleague Meek and the Uphoffs. Also to Hans Heckmann who has done a beautiful job to spread ITC information.

You know by experience, Mark, how dangerous drugs of all kinds can be. Try to warn humanity that they not only alter their present lives on your side, but also influence in a harmful way their future lives. Go on with your ITC experiments and you will see that the bridge to the States will soon be strengthened.

Regina, as your twin soul, can help you. Listen to her Inner Voice and you will be guided in the right way.

TECHNICIAN: End of contact.

After the contact we returned to the table to play the tape back, phrase by phrase, to decipher what Konstantin had said. Most paranormal messages over radio are not as clear as those coming through the telephone receiver.

After we had transcribed the contact, Jules made a copy of a recent phone dialogue with American ragtime composer Scott Joplin to present to his American guests.

SCOTT JOPLIN, JEANNETTE MEEK, AND HER DOG TERRY

This recent contact occurred when a friend, Hilde Schwickerath, visited Maggy. Hilde's husband, Otto, had just died. Unknown to the two ladies, Scott Joplin was with Otto in the spirit world. Otto had a message for his wife and Scott was going to convey it over the phone. As is often the case, it was a short, simple message—an obscure little fact that only the Schwickerath couple knew anything about.

Unfortunately, in this case, Hilde didn't recall the incident. Add to that the fact that she and Maggy speak limited English and so they had a hard time understanding Scott's Black American dialect, plus Scott's growing frustration in trying to get a rather silly little message across.

In the actual taped dialogue—which was more a comedy of errors—were all the problems of communicating between dimensions. Listening, we felt Scott's frustrations. After all, he'd been away from the Earth for seventy-five years, and all the problems

of the spoken word obviously irritated him. This was
the first time Scott had spoken over the phone from
the spirit world, and it took him a few times before he
could even say "Hello."

MAGGY: Hallo?

SCOTT: H'lwha.

MAGGY: Hallo?

SCOTT: H'lwha.

MAGGY: Hallo?

SCOTT: (The words run together) Hello-I'm-Scott-
Joplin.

MAGGY: (She asks him in German to identify
himself)

SCOTT: Scott Joplin. Joplin, Scott—can you hear
me?

MAGGY: Chaplain, yes, I can hear you.

SCOTT: Okay, I got here with me...

MAGGY: (Suddenly remembering an earlier
contact in which Scott Joplin was mentioned as a
friend of Jeannette Meek) Ah, Mr. Joplin!

SCOTT: Yeah! I got here with me an Otto
Schwickerath. He says something about Sanc
Johanna Marcht or something like that. Sanc
Johanna Marcht in Saarbrucken. Sanc Johanna
Marcht in Saarbrucken, and a *bause* on his head.
You got me?

MAGGY: No, I haven't got you. What do you call
her?

SCOTT: Uh... Herr Schwickerath—Schwickerath...

MAGGY: Schwickerath, yes. (Maggy turns the
phone over to Hilde, still not realizing that Otto
Schwickerath was with Scott Joplin.)

SCOTT: ... the name ....

HILDE: I'm here. I hear you.

SCOTT: Yeah, okay. He tells me something about Sanc Joanna Marcht, or something like that.

HILDE: Sanc Johann?

SCOTT: Johanna Marcht of Saarbrucken.

HILDE (NODDING): Ja, Ja, you can find in Saarbrucken, Sanc Johanna Marcht!

SCOTT: Yeah, okay, he tells me about a *bause*, but I don't know what it is, "*bause*." (A *bause* is a bump on the head in a dialect of Southern Germany.)

HILDE: Bowser? It's a name? Bowser?

SCOTT: Not Bowser. He spells it b-a-u-s-e. *Bause*.

HILDE: Ah, *bause*.

SCOTT: Like a boil on his head. That's a boil on his head.

(*Beule* is a more general German term for a bump, pronounced "boil-uh," and there's indication that Scott has it confused with a boil, an infected, swollen area of the body.)

HILDE: Mm-hm.

SCOTT: Got me?

HILDE: I don't know.

SCOTT: (sighs in obvious frustration)

HILDE: What means it? Hello?

SCOTT: Hello?

HILDE: What's your name?

SCOTT: (a bit flabergasted now) JOPLIN—SCOTT JOPLIN!

HILDE: Chapel? (Then in the background, Maggy tells her it's Scott Joplin). Ah, Joplin. Eh, do I know you?

SCOTT: No, you don't know me.

HILDE: Oh? Never?

SCOTT: I don't think so, Lady.

(Hilde and Maggy talk a moment in German, and Maggy mentions that Scott and Hilde are both friends of Jeannette Meek.)

HILDE: Ah, Jeannette Meek is your friend?

SCOTT: Yes, yes, my pal-friend. Yeah.

HILDE: Ah, my husband is Otto Schwickerath. Do you know him?

SCOTT: Yes, certainly.

HILDE: (mutters something in German)

SCOTT: That guy's standing here.

HILDE: (with deep emotion) Ah! Otto is here? Oh greetings. A lot of greetings!

SCOTT: A bause, he's saying it's called a boil.

HILDE: Uh, Maggy is hearing now, yes?

MAGGY: Hello, here is Maggy again.

SCOTT: (in distress now) Ah, see there, it's all rather stupid, I think. A *bause*, a *beule*, he said. A *beule* on the head.

MAGGY: A *beule* on the head?

SCOTT: Yeah, a *beule*.

MAGGY: A *beule* on the head, what do you mean by that?

SCOTT Your grandfather says, "A *knup*."

(A *knup* or *knubbel* is a knock on the head, or a very hard lump. Evidently, Maggy's deceased grandfather has gotten into the conversation, as well.)

MAGGY: A *knup*? *Knup*? Yes. And what is a ....

(Scott is getting frustrated with the whole thing, which means that the contact will end soon unless things can be resolved.

MAGGY: (In soothing voice) It's okay, there's somebody here who can understand.

SCOTT: Okay, fine.

MAGGY: (Trying to sound cheerful) Okay, fine! Thank you, Mr. Joplin. It's very nice ….

SCOTT: (regaining his composure) It's nice to talk to you."

MAGGY: Yes, it's nice to talk to you! Uh, Mr. Joplin, can you tell me anything about Jeannette Meek?

(A dog apparently comes close to Scott now. Its yapping is audible)

SCOTT: A terrier here. Here's the dog. That's the dog.

MAGGY: Hello? I hear the dog. What dog is it?"

SCOTT: Terry.

(More than one clairvoyant colleague has reported seeing a small, squarish, Scotty-like dog moving around at the feet of Jeannette Meek since her transition to spirit. Jeannette has told mediums that the dog's name is Terry.)

MAGGY: Terry?

SCOTT: He's together with Kucki. (The deceased dog Kucki had belonged to Hilde, who now hears the dog and gets back on the phone.)

HILDE: Ah, hello. Is this Berta or is this Kucki?

SCOTT: (exasperated): I already told Maggy it's Kucki. I told her. Do you folks communicate? ….

It was unfortunate that Scott Joplin, having been away from Earth for seventy-five years, was chosen to relay such a dubious message. However, it's apparent that returning to the problems posed by spoken communication can be a very difficult and frustrating experience for someone in the higher planes.

(Jeannette Meek and Scott Joplin seem to have similar "home frequencies" in either the very high astral planes or the mental-causal planes. They, like Dr. Konstantin Raudive, must "commute down" to the mid-astral planes to participate in ITC).

As far as communicating information across dimensions, this wasn't a particularly useful contact. Still, the failed attempt to get a simple message across reveals a lot to us about life on the other side.

For one thing, our pets can accompany us. Also, it's evident that we carry our tempers and frustration levels along with us. Life in "Heaven" isn't all clouds and roses.

Furthermore, contacts such as this one are not just between two people. Just as Scott is together with Otto Schwickerath and Maggy's grandfather (and probably a few others as well), other contacts have indicated the presence of friends accompanying the spirit communicator.

The main mode of communication in the spirit worlds is telepathy, in which concepts and images are shared rather clearly. When our friends get involved in ITC and have to revert to words and phrases with all their inherent difficulties and potential misunderstandings, they obviously have troubles.

A LETTER FROM JULES VERNE

Also, during our trip to Luxembourg, the Harsch-Fischbachs gave us a picture of Jules Verne which they'd received via computer recently from their spirit colleagues along with a letter from the famous French science fiction writer. They'd received these items shortly before leaving for a Parisian ITC Congress and were asked by their spirit colleagues to present them to the French people.

(Translated from French to English by Greta Avedisian):

It is not without emotion that I am writing these few lines, destined, from what I have just been told, to be presented at the time of a conference in my homeland—France—as well as in Paris where I was, if my memories serve me right, for the final time in the winter of 1896/97, nearly one hundred years ago, according to your calculation of time.

Permit me first to present myself: My name is Jules Verne, and I suppose it is not unknown to you, since it already had a certain golden glow at the time I was living. Indeed, and as strange as this might seem to you, I am good and dead, and yet as alive as you are, if not more so.

I here state: deaf in the left ear, practically blind and cardiac, in possession of a deficient stomach and suffering from rheumatism, with acute gout and diabetes, I was startled to find myself, at the expiration of my earthly life on the 24th of March, 1905, transported from my domicile at Six Boulevard Longueville, as it were, without warning and without my being exactly able to describe the circumstances, towards a place that was totally strange to me.

I suddenly realized with amazement that I no longer had pain anywhere, and that my blindness had completely disappeared, which allowed me to observe, among other things, that I was in a sumptuous palace bringing to mind the splendid residences of the rajahs, with walls constructed not in sandstone but in resplendent white marble. The opulence of the many mirrors reflected the blaze of the solid silver furniture. The mural paintings showed courtiers and girls who were dancing, and I noticed a pleasant freshness emanating from a number of little fountains surrounding luxuriant green plants. My hearing, now completely restored, finally permitted me once more to savor the melodious warble of the countless birds.

I then heard music so soft and sweet that I cried with joy. Slender, fine and exquisite creatures, reminding me of my Honorine when she still possessed all the beauty and freshness of her youth, and who, molded in their orange and blue silk cloths which contrasted with their tanned skin, invited me to sit upon the soft pillows and inquired as to my desires and wishes.

They spoke to me in a language that up until then I had never heard, but strangely, I understood immediately—and I was even able to answer them in the same idiom. (It was only later that I was informed that it was the "Language of the River" that each one acquires as soon as one arrive here.

For a long time I thought I was dreaming, and it was only after weeks and months—which somehow seemed to me to pass like the flight of swallows—that I finally understood that I was deceased.

Naturally, I searched for friends and acquaintances who were with me during my Earthly life. Not one of the Hetzels, nor my dear parents Sophie and Pierre were, unfortunately, known in the palace nor in the agglomerations situated in the clearings of the majestic forests that surrounded my new domicile. I never saw a gardener touch or trim these trees or shrubs, which gracefully seemed to adjust their spacing themselves. It even seemed to me that they themselves destroyed the weeds surrounding them by the generations of some enzyme that dissolved the matter and produced some sort of compost.

But I am getting lost in details, a character trait I have in common with Dickens and Balzac, my favorite authors.

Alas! All beauty, even that which I discovered in Kwapore—for that is what my new home was named—ends in numbing the soul, and perfection is often the symbol of stagnation.

It is only recently that I have gotten wind of the existence of the group Timestream, and still only due to chance. One of the many passing travelers at Kwapore and with whom I was conversing on a gentle night of the full moon on terrace decked with "*jalis*," a certain Arthur Moos, a handsome man with thoughtful face, confided to me—his tongue no doubt loosened by the dry wine accompanying the slices of marrow of a fish with pale pink flesh—confided that he had quit the group of researchers in transcommunication (the word was new to me) because he was embarrassed by some sort of blunder made by his wife, still on Earth. He now wandered and searched through the valley of the River, poor wretch, in search of a new hearth. This Arthur reports that my nephew Gaston, son of my dear brother Paul, joined this group in contact with Luxembourg. (The poor boy had spent a few years in a nursing home there where he had "died" in the course of one of the great wars that, I am told, had ravaged Europe after 1910.)

Three companions who were with me at the table in the palace, had likewise heard of him: two Englishmen who both had died in London—one a Nathaniel Wopping having perished at the time of the great fire of 1666 and the other James Smurl, dying of a hemorrhage during the bombardments of a world war. The third was an Indian who claimed to be the former Rajah of Bikaner, but it would be difficult for me to say if it is true or not. In any case, if he is not of princely descent, he possesses the manners and the style.

A fascinating air voyage brought all four of us here (this time the experiment with the "giant" balloon succeeded!) to be beside the beautiful Swejen and her colleagues of Timestream.

So here I am, my French friends—and others of course—ready to attempt the experiment to establish a bridge between our world and you, the French researchers.

Be assured: I am in good company. Among throngs of others, Michel Kisacanin, the grandfather of (French experimenter) Monique Simonet as well as the ex-marshal Sebestiano Porta, already involved in this work before my arrival, are all of valuable help to me. (Note to Father Francois Brune: I am going to buckle up like a Breton.) My first message has become long and I know it, but it is a vice I share with another new friend here—Konrad Lorenz. He, too, never knows when to quit!

Jules Verne

The communication from Jules Verne is not only entertaining, but instructive as well, in many ways. He is obviously living in a palace he has mentally created. For some reason, he is separated from his parents and his "beloved Honorine." Are there Karmic circumstances for this separation? Did Honorine no longer wish to be with him? Have his parents already incarnated or moved up to another dimension? Or, are they in a lower dimension?

Most significant about the late author's communication is that although the palace is very beautiful, he's dissatisfied with it and describes it as a "stasis" or "numbing of the soul." It is this dissatisfaction with a "perfect situation" that encourages a person to reincarnate to experience new situations. Already, Jules Verne, an adventurous man, is seeking new friends and new experiences at Timestream. Who knows what will come of this fortunate collaboration.

At any rate, I [Mark Macy] had a fine time in Luxembourg in the summer of 94—Juliet Hollister, Alison van Dyk, and I renewed friendships across the Atlantic and made new ones across the veil! Being inclined toward music and writing from a young age, I was especially touched by the closeness I suddenly felt toward Scott Joplin and Jules Verne.

I returned to the States more convinced than ever that ITC is among the most vital fields of research underway today, bridging the physical to the spiritual and shedding light on a healthy future for a troubled planet.

This is just the beginning, my friends, just the beginning.

Photo Section

★ ERNST MACKES/ 04-03-1993

Plate 1—Ernst Mackes. Ernst and Margret Mackes were very close friends with the Luxembourg experimenters, Maggy and Jules Harsch, and were determined that their friendship would last beyond the grave. Margret died in April 1987 and, true to her intent, stayed in contact with her husband and their friends by sending messages occasionally through the ITC equipment at CETL. Ernst died on November 26, 1992, got settled into his new home, and within months delivered two long letters and this picture through the computer of Maggy and Jules.

Plate 2—Swejen Salter. ITC project leader Dr. Swejen Salter is shown in part of her laboratory at the Timestream sending station located in the mid-astral planes of the spirit world, what Frederick Myers called the "plane of illusion" because the forms and structures in that realm are created by the collective thoughts, beliefs and memories of its inhabitants, with the help of higher beings. Dr. Salter, born in 1949, died in 1987 and from the spirit world quickly took a leading role in the young field of ITC unfolding on Earth.

georgecukorpresentsapictureofthoma
salvaedisonsacannerdebythenethodde
veloppedbytinestream/actuallyatthe
monentofthissnapshot/t.a.edisonisa
bout3.oocmilesawayatthestaionofthe
oerehouse/thepictureofjeannettenee
kuilfollowinafewdays/
read:operahousandstation/
both/georgecukorandthonasedisonare
closefriendsofklausschreiberwhouor
kstogetherwiththeninordertoino=pro
/readinordertoimprovepicturequalit

greetingstoallfriendsoftimestream/swejensalter/projectdirector/19-04-91/10
:23

Plate 3—Thomas Edison and George Cukor. This picture of two well-known US figures—inventor Thomas Edison (died 1931) and filmmaker George Cukor (died 1983) arrived in Luxembourg on April 19, 1991, with the following message: "George Cukor presents a picture of Thomas Alva Edison scanned by the methods developed by Timestream. Actually at the moment of this snapshot, T.A. Edison is about 3,000 miles away from the station at the opera house. The picture of Jeannette Meek will follow in a few days. Both George Cukor and Thomas Edison are close friends of Klaus Schreiber who works together with them in order to improve picture quality."

Plate 4—Henri Sainte Claire de Ville. This man was born in 1818 in the Antilles and later became a chemistry professor and inventor in France. He was in contact with a team of American experimenters led by George Meek (Project Lifeline) in the 1980s, and made contact with the Harsch team in Luxembourg in 1986 during a Transatlantic experiment between the two ITC groups. Mssr. de Ville delivered several voice messages through the Luxembourg equipment and sent a short video sequence showing himself in his astral body, turning his head. This is one frame from that video sequence.

Plate 5—Albert Einstein. After his death, Albert Einstein chose to stay in touch with the Earth by sending telepathic messages to many mediumistic people, including experimenter Klaus Schreiber of Germany, a pioneer in ITC work. In the mid-1980s Schreiber was receiving numerous images of loved ones and well- known people across his television, including this picture of Einstein. Since then, Schreiber has made his transition and now continues ITC work from the other side of the veil.

Plate 6—Klaus Schreiber in lifetime. This is German ITC experimenter Klaus Schreiber in his lab in 1986. His final years on Earth were not especially pleasant ones, as many of his family members met untimely deaths from illness and accidents. His grief and longing apparently provided some of the emotional energy required to enable the phenomenal contacts he received across his television during this troubled period.

Plate 7—Klaus Schreiber in his astral body. After his transition, Schreiber began sending pictures and messages to his colleagues whom he had left behind on Earth, including this picture of himself, which he sent to the Harsch couple in Luxembourg.

Plate 8—Friedrich Juergenson during lifetime. In 1959, Swedish filmmaker Friedrich Juergenson captured spirit voices on tape while taping bird songs. Amazed, he was soon taping thousands of these voices to become a pioneer in what has come to be called EVP, or electronic voice phenomenon. This is Juergenson several years before his death in 1987.

Plate 9—F. Juergenson in his etheric body. Juergenson was psychically gifted, a characteristic typical of the most successful experimenters in EVP and ITC. Before, during and after his death he maintained a close telepathic rapport with his friend Claude Thorlin. On the day he died, Juergenson issued a silent message to his friend Thorlin that he (Juergenson) would try, during his own funeral ceremony, to manifest an image of himself on his friend's TV. So, while most of Juergenson's loved ones were at his funeral, Thorlin was at home, capturing this picture of his old friend with a Polaroid camera. As explained in Chapter 5, after we die we live in our etheric body, usually for just a few days. This is the spirit body we associate with ghosts and apparitions.

Plate 10—S. Salter sending F. Juergenson's picture to Earth. This picture was received by the Luxembourg experimenters Maggy and Jules Harsch in 1992 as a computer-scanned image. It was planted on their computer disk at the couple's home while they were out. It shows ITC project director Swejen Salter *in her lab in the spirit world* with a portrait in her computer of Friedrich Juergenson in his astral body.

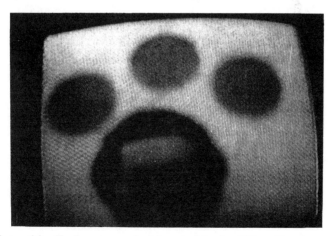

Plate 11—F. Juergenson in his astral body. This video image was received in Germany at about the same time that the computer- scanned image in Plate 10 was received in Luxembourg. Simulcasts of this type are becoming more common as our spirit friends take extra efforts to show the legitimacy of ITC to a skeptical public.

Plate 12—Konstantin Raudive. These pictures show ITC pioneer Konstantin Raudive in his physical body at middle age (left) and in his astral body 13 years after death in 1974 (right). He was a main figure in EVP work before his death, collecting over 70,000 voices on tape and writing the book Breakthrough. Since his death he says it is his calling to help EVP and ITC experimenters get better contacts on Earth. In 1994 experimenters in seven countries reported getting telephone calls from Raudive. That included five experimenters in the US. This book's author (Mark Macy) received three calls in his home in January and February of that year.

Plate 13—Pierre Klein. The image on the right is the first paranormal video picture received by the Luxembourg experimenters. It shows a young acquaintance of theirs, Pierre Klein, who had recently made his transition to spirit. To the left, Pierre is shown as he had appeared on Earth. He happened to be in a train when this photo was taken. The spirit image to the right is indicative of the low-quality images the Harsch couple were receiving early in their experiments.

Plate 14—Sir Richard Francis Burton (1821-1890). Early in their experiments, the Luxembourg team frequently heard a deep voice with an English accent. Eventually the intelligence behind the voice identified himself as Sir Richard Francis Burton, the 19th-Century explorer who had translated "1,001 Arabian Nights" into English. This picture came across the Harsch couple's television in 1987, early in their video experiments.

Plate 15—Hanna Buschbeck. German experimenter Hanna Buschbeck founded the German Electronic Voice Association in the 1960s to provide a means of networking and documentation for the many EVP experimenters in Europe. This picture of Hanna Buschbeck came across the television in 1987, not long after her funeral. She is once again a young woman, smiling to her friends on Earth.

Plate 16—Ezra Braun during lifetime. This picture of Ezra Braun was taken in August 1985, a year before he died at age 11 of leukemia. During his final months on Earth, solace came from the European TV programs about ITC and EVP experimenting. His parents promised to try to contact him by tape, and he didn't cry after that.

Ezra BRAUN am 19.08.1985

Plate 17—Ezra Braun in spirit. Ezra died in the fall of 1986, and by 1991 he was working with the spirit group Timestream, who sent this picture of the young man, now obviously delighted with his new life on the astral planes. Ezra works with 16th-Century physician Paracelsus. Their group sends medical information to Earth.

Plate 18—Paracelsus. Theophrastus von Hohenheim (1493-1541), better known as Paracelsus, was a well-known physician, Naturist and philosopher, who is now making contact with Earth through various channels, including the ITC lab in Luxembourg, where this picture arrived in 1992. It shows Paracelsus with the view from the balcony of his home on the astral planes. While on Earth he had once said, "After my death I shall accomplish more for you than before."

Plate 19—George and Jeannette Meek. This picture shows the Meeks during a trip to Egypt in the early 1980s. Since Jeannette's death in 1990, they have enjoyed more than 100 dialogs across dimensions. George is regarded by many to be one of the fathers of modern ITC because of the Spiricom device which he helped his associate Bill O'Neil to develop in 1980, providing the first extended dialog with spirit beings.

Plate 20—Jeannette Meek in "the Summerland." This computer-scanned image, received in Luxembourg in November 1992, shows Jeannette, her daughter Nancy Carol, and filmmaker Hal Roach, all of whom reside in the higher spiritual levels of the astral planes. A computer message from Hal Roach that accompanied the picture ended with the note: "The best boy assembling this picture: Frank Blehle." Later, this book's author (Mark Macy) learned that "best boy" is a term commonly used in Hollywood to refer to people behind the scenes in the filmmaking industry who take care of the technical aspects of film production.

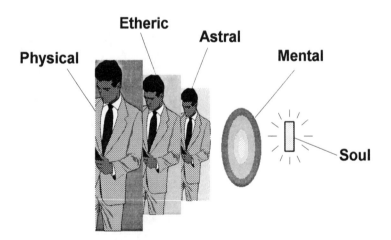

Plate 21—Our multidimensional nature. When we die and shed the physical body, we live in the etheric body for a few days, then cast off that body as well. Then we live in an astral body which is a subtle version of our physical body at age 25-35. Eventually our human form melts into formlessness, and we are no longer a human being, but a light being whose life centers around love and wisdom. Finally, we shed the mental sheaths and, as a soul, merge with God.

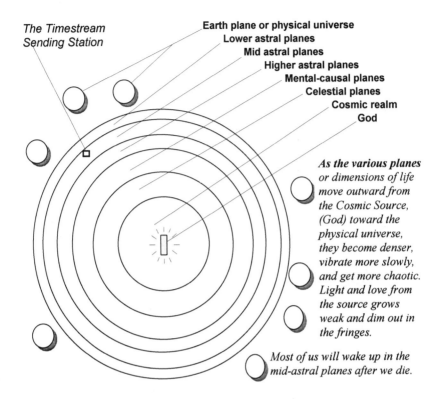

The Timestream Sending Station

Earth plane or physical universe
Lower astral planes
Mid astral planes
Higher astral planes
Mental-causal planes
Celestial planes
Cosmic realm
God

As the various planes or dimensions of life move outward from the Cosmic Source, (God) toward the physical universe, they become denser, vibrate more slowly, and get more chaotic. Light and love from the source grows weak and dim out in the fringes.

Most of us will wake up in the mid-astral planes after we die.

Plate 22—Our multidimensional omniverse. These various dimensions, or planes of reality, all exist in the same space but remain distinct by the frequency or vibratory rate of their substance, like radio and TV signals jumbled together in a room yet remaining distinct by their frequency. The *physical plane*, or material universe, is the outer fringe of the spiritual omniverse. Frederick Myers called it the first human plane. The *lower astral plane*, or second human plane, has also been called the Interim, Hell, Hades and Purgatory. *The mid-astral plane*, or third human plane, is where most of us will wind up after we die and shed the physical body. It is a nice, Earth-like existence. Myers called this the plane of illusion because it is like a dream world. The *higher astral plane* (fourth human plane) is the realm which most Christians call "Heaven" and what spiritualists call "the Summerland." Myers called this the plane of colors or world of forms ("Eidos"). The *mental-causal plane* (fifth plane), or what Myers called the plane of flames, is where the spirit loses its human appearance and takes on a flame-like appearance. Reality here is created by the thoughts of the inhabitants. The *celestial plane* (sixth plane), or plane of light, is beyond the scope of human languages to describe. It is a realm of pure thought. The *cosmic plane* (seventh plane) is where the soul merges with the Source, or God. It retains its individuality yet finds a oneness with all souls.

Plate 23—Angie Mreche. Had she lived into adulthood, Angie Mreche would have been the aunt of ITC experimenter Maggie Harsch. Apparently her life was typical of that of many higher beings who incarnate on Earth as highly sensitive people. It is not an easy life, but much can be learned by them. At the same time, much can be learned *from* them by those who have the good fortune to cross paths with these higher beings while they spend time on Earth. After all, among the ranks of these higher beings are the great prophets and spiritual teachers who have walked the Earth down through the ages.

Bibliography

Banding, Peter. *Voices from the Tapes*. New York: Drake Publishers, 1973.

Brinkley, Dannion. *Saved by the Light*. New York: Villard Books, 1994

Eadie, Betty J. *Embraced by the Light*. Placerville, Ca.: Gold Leaf Press, 1992.

Farthing, Geoffrey. *Exploring the Great Beyond*. Wheaton: The Theosophical Publishing House, 1978.

Fiore, Charles & Alan Landsburg. *Death Encounters*. New York: Bantam Books, 1979.

Ford, Arthur. *Nothing so Strange*. New York: Harper & Row, 1958.

Ford, Arthur. *The Life Beyond Death*. New York: G.P. Putnam's Sons, 1971.

Ford, Arthur. *Unknown But Known*. New York: Evanston, Harper & Row, 1968.

Head, Joseph & S.L. Cranston. *Reincarnation: The Phoenix Fire Mystery*. New York: Warner Books, 1979.

Kubler-Ross, Elisabeth. *On Death and Dying*. New York: Macmillan Publishing Co., Inc., 1969.

Martin, Joel & Patricia Romanowski. *We Don't Die*. New York: The Berkley Publishing Group, 1988.

Meek, George W.. *After We Die, What then?* Columbus: Ariel Press, 1987

Meek, George W.. *From Enigma to Science*. Columbus: Ariel Press, 1973

Mitchell, Edgar D. *Psychic Exploration, a Challenge for Science*. New York: G.P. Putnam's Sons, a Capricorn Book, 1976.

Monroe, Robert A.. *Journeys out of the Body*. New York: Doubleday & Company, Inc., 1971.

Monroe, Robert A.. *Far Journeys*. New York: Doubleday & Company, Inc., 1985.

Monroe, Robert A.. *Ultimate Journey*. New York: Doubleday, 1994.

Montgomery, Ruth. *Here and Hereafter*. New York: Ballantine (a Fawcett Crest Book), 1968.

Moody, Raymond A.. *Life After Life*. New York: Bantam Books, 1975.

Moody, Raymond. A.A. *Reflections on Life after Life*. New York, Bantam Books, 1978.

Moody, Raymond A.. *The Light Beyond, New Explorations*. New York: Bantam, 1988.

Morse, Melvin. *Closer to the Light*. New York: Ivy Books, 1990.

Moss, Thelma. *The Probability of the Impossible*. New York: New American Library (a Plume Book), 1974.

Myers, F.W.H.. *Human Personality and its Survival of Bodily Death*. New York: University Books, Inc. 1961.

Myers, John. *Voices from the Edge of Eternity*. New York: Pyramid Books, 1973.

Osis, Karlis & Erlandur Haraldsson. *At the Hour of Death*. New York: Avon Books, 1977.

Ostrander, Sheila & Lynn Schroeder. *Handbook of Psi Discoveries*. New York: Berkley Publishing Corp., 1974.

Raudive, Konstantin. *Breakthrough, Electronic Communication with the Dead may be Possible*. New York: Zebra Books, 1971.

Bibliography

Ritchie, George G. *Return from Tomorrow*. Waco, Tx.: Chosen Books, 1923.

Steiner, Rudolf. *Life Between Death and Rebirth*. Spring Valley, New York: Anthroposophic Press, Inc., 1968.

Stevenson, Ian. *Twenty Cases Suggestive of Reincarnation*. New York: American Society for Psychical Research, 1966.

Wambach, Helen. *Life Before Life*. New York: Bantam Books, 1979.

Wambach, Helen. *Reliving Past Lives*. New York: Harper & Row, 1978.

Weiss, Brian L.. *Many Lives, Many Masters*. New York: Simon & Schuster Inc., 1988.

Weiss, Brian L. *Through Time into Healing*. New York: Simon & Schuster Inc., 1992.

White, Stewart Edward. *The Betty Book*. New York: E.P. Dutton, 1977.

White, Stewart Edward. *The Unobstructed Universe*. New York: Dell Publishing Co., Inc., 1968.

Whitton, Joel L. & Joe Fisher. *Life Between Life*. New York: Doubleday & Company., Inc. (a Dolphin Book), 1986.

ABOUT THE AUTHORS

PAT KUBIS

She has a Ph.D. in Comparative Literature from the University of California at Riverside, with a minor in philosophy. An English professor for 23 years, she has studied Yoga for over 20 years with American mystic and author, Paramahansa Ramakrishna Ananda, and taught parapsychology on a college level.

She is a free lance writer, having written articles for the *Los Angeles Times*, a novelist, and a TV scriptwriter. Her special interest is "life after death" and she has an immense library on the subject. She studied yoga for over thirty-two years and has left her body innumerable times and traveled to the astral plane. Her metaphysical life began at fifteen when, at Hollywood High School, she had her first out-of-body experience. From that time, she was able to leave her body and travel to other dimensions.

As various dear ones in her life made the transition, she either saw them at the time of death or immediately after, and she also traveled to the astral plane to see them. Her mother, Suenina Henion, died August 28, 1977, and Pat kept in contact with her for over two years, often visiting her on the astral plane. In fact, her mother called her on the telephone a day after she died. Pat STILL is in touch both in dream and in meditation with the man she wanted very much to marry, and has visited him on the astral plane many times.

About seven years ago, in one of her meditations, she left her body and voyaged to a locale beyond the earth. She saw the earth in full color, exactly as Carl Gustav Jung had written about in his autobiography, and found herself in a conference room. The room had a domed ceiling and great curved windows. About fifteen people came into the room and everyone there seemed to know her. She knew she had come here to work on a mutual project. But when she returned to her body, she couldn't remember what the project was!

In 1993, as she read through the research on ITC, one of the reports mentioned the conference room in which Swejen Salter, Director of Timestream, met with higher beings to discuss Timestream's mission. Pat had the eerie sensation this was the same conference room she had visited ten years before, out-of-body. Was it this particular project that had been talked about? Had she indeed been there? If so, she perhaps was the writer for the project.

She decided to write Maggy Harsch-Fischbach, Director of the Luxembourg Lab, to ask Swejen Salter (the Director of Timestream on the astral plane) to confirm that she (Pat) had met in the council room with Salter. Shortly after, she received a fax in German that had been sent to Mark Macy who translates the research.

The fax said: "Pat Kubis is right. She was in the council room in an out-of-body trip." The fax told Mark that Pat could be trusted with all research information. But the last line of the fax electrified Pat. It said: "Richard versogt Quink (Richard takes care of Quink)." Quink was a jet black cat that had lived with

Pat for over 18 years and had died several years before.

Excited, Pat called Mark to find out who "Richard" was. Mark replied that it was Sir Richard Francis Burton, the well known explorer. Mark had had no idea of what a "Quink" was until Pat explained it was the name of her cat.

The fax to Mark Macy, confirming Pat's out-of-body visit to the council room, opened the door to Mark and Pat's collaboration on this book. But what delighted Pat the most was that her much loved cat-friend was now voyaging the astral plane with Sir. Richard Francis Burton—and incidentally, Quink had loved to travel and logged many earth miles in an RV.

MARK MACY

He is a researcher, writer, and lecturer in subjects of peace, healing, life after death and spiritual reality. His chief focus since 1991 has been on the field of ITC, or instrumental transcommunication, the use of electronic instruments to get long messages and clear images from intelligent minds residing in nonphysical dimensions—so-called spirits of the dead. Today he works closely with the American ITC pioneer, George Meek, and with leading researchers in Europe. He conducts ITC experiments with a small group of researchers in Colorado and gives workshops and presentations around the country to educate others about ITC. He writes articles and books on ITC and spirituality.

Mark was not always spiritually inclined. Until 1988 his main interests were systems thinking and world peace. He conferred with leading thinkers in many countries, compiled international anthologies that took a systems approach to planetary healing, and gave lectures on his findings.

Then he developed colon cancer which not only brought him very close to death, but also signaled that it was time to take a new direction onto a more spiritual path. As is the case with many people in today's hurried world, Mark had lost touch with his spirit and his true purpose for living on Earth.

For a time Mark became devoted to two spiritual mentors, a Hindu master named Gurumayi Chidvilasananda whose teachings kick-started his soul, and Dr. Bernie Siegel whose books on love and healing helped open his heart. Mark began attending conferences to explore inwardly into the soul instead of outwardly into the world. But even then he believed that when we die, that's it. Some analytic little cell in his brain seemed to need physical evidence of spiritual existence and continuing life before he could broaden his view beyond the physical world. Then Mark ran into leading-edge spiritual thinker, George Meek, at one of the conferences. When George presented spirit pictures, a computer letter that his wife Jeannette had sent to him several months after her funeral, and a roadmap of the spirit worlds, the information almost knocked Mark out of his seat. He developed an instant, insatiable hunger for more information.

The two men exchanged several letters after that conference, and before long they decided to collaborate on some books, to start Continuing Life Research, and to launch their new spiritual enterprise with a trip to Europe to visit the leading experimenters. That trip led Mark not only into a Transatlantic friendship with Maggy and Jules Harsch-Fischbach of Luxembourg, the world's leading ITC experimenters, but also into a transdimensional association with a well-organized team of light-hearted, enthusiastic spirit colleagues who call their spirit-world research group *Timestream*.

The Timestream group includes deceased experimenters (Konstantin Raudive of Latvia, Friedrich Juergenson of Sweden, Klaus Schreiber of Germany, Bill O'Neil of the US), well-known historic figures (16th-Century father of holistic medicine Paracelsus, 17th-Century explorer Sir Richard Francis Burton, 19th-Century inventor Henri Sainte Claire de Ville, Eleanor Roosevelt, Thomas Edison, Nikola Tesla, and Dr. Marie Curie), recently deceased celebrities (movie producer Hal Roach, director George Cukor, actor Michael Landon, and philosopher Rudolf Carnap), and many deceased friends and relatives.

To say that Mark has enlarged his circle of friends in the past few years would be an understatement. To say he has friends around the world would also be an understatement.

Mark has a bachelor's degree in journalism and extensive training and experience in computers, telecommunications and electronics, which turns out to be a good combination for ITC reporting and research.

CERTIFICATE

TO WHOM IT MAY CONCERN :

THIS IS TO CERTIFY THAT

MR. MARK MACY , CONTINUING LIFE Foundation Inc., USA

IS HEREWITH INVESTED WITH AUTHORITY TO PRESENT ANY RESEARCH MATERIAL MADE ACCESSIBLE TO HIM BY THE

CERCLE D'ETUDES sur la TRANSCOMMUNICATION a.s.b.l.

LUXEMBOURG - EUROPE.

MR. MACY ACTS AS A FREELANCE COLLABORATOR OF CETL AND ONLY WITH THE INTENTION TO SPREAD THE EXISTENCE OF THE PHENOMENON OF TRANSCOMMUNICATION IN THE UNITED STATES OF AMERICA. IT IS UP TO HIM TO DECIDE WHATEVER HE INTENDS TO PUBLISH IN ARTICLES, BOOKS OR CONFERENCES. HE HAS NO FEES TO PAY TO CETL FOR HIS WORK.

LUXEMBOURG, ON THE NINTH OF OCTOBER 1992

MAGGY HARSCH-FISCHBACH
PRESIDENT OF CETL

Additional Information About

Continuing Life Research

We Survive!
Incredible Experiments in Life After Death

A book by George Meek and Mark Macy
Winter 1995

This book encapsulates the major findings of George Meek's 25 years of research into spiritual reality and the basic nature of Man. In the first two chapters we get a clearer view of our spiritual nature and our multidimensional universe than ever before possible through the five senses, thanks to "road maps" that illustrate the spiritual realms, and actual photos of spiritual energies and spirit bodies.

We are drawn into the personal lives of George and Jeannette Meek during the difficult months leading up to her physical death in 1990, following a series of strokes. We share their telepathic conversations while Jeannette lay on her deathbed, unable to speak. Those dialogs continued once Jeannette had moved into the next world. There she encounters their daughter Nancy Carol, who had died in infancy, and befriends Eleanor Roosevelt, Scott Joplin and other well-known personalities.

This book explores the many possibilities that await us all in the next life. It explores the fate of the planet, as well, in this time of earthly changes.

For more information contact
Continuing Life Research
P.O. Box 11036,
Boulder CO 80301, USA,
(303) 673-0660.

Breakthrough II: More Experiments in Electronic Communication with the Dead

A book by Dr. Theo Locher and Maggy Horsch-Fischbach
English version translated by Hans Heclkmann.
Edited by Mark Macy
Spring 1996

This book emerges from the heart of ITC research in Europe and provides an up-close look at recent events in modern parapsychology. It explores the successes of well-known experimenters George Meek and William O'Neil of the United States, Marcello Bacci of Italy, and Manfred Boden, Hans-Otto Koening, Peter and Gisela Heartins, Klaus Schreiber, Adoff Homes and Friedrich Malkhoff of Germany. It describes particularly the work of Maggy and Jules Harsch-Fischbach of Luxembourg. The book also explores the dangers involved in spiritual communication, and ways to avoid them.

Orthodox Christians and scientists alike have incomplete information about the next life. Neither the models of modern physics, biology or psychology, nor the well-aged pages of religious texts can fully account for the phenomena occurring today among the world's ITC researchers.

We think of this book as a modern-day sequel to the book *Breakthrough,* by ITC pioneer Konstantm Raudive—a leading figure working with us from the other side.

For more information contact
Continuing Life Research
P.O. Box 11036,
Boulder CO 80301, USA,
(303) 673-0660.

CETL INFOnews

A journal published in Luxembourg by Jules and Maggy Harsch-Fischbach, the world's leading ITC experimenters.

English version translated by Hans Heckmann.
Edited and published by Mark Macy

This journal, published since 1986, provides detailed reports on the astonishing contacts being made by experimenters at Cercle d'Etudes sur la Transcom-munication—Luxembourg (CETL).

ITC Newsletter

Edited by Mark Macy
Beginning Winter, 1995-96

Continuing Life Research will publish this quarterly digest to document the most recent ITC contacts. Published under the auspicis of the international ITC organization. This organization will provide stability and cooperation in the study and practice of ITC which, our spirit colleagues have informed us, will strengthen the contact bridge for future research.

The Miracle of ITC

An audio tape by Continuing Life Research describing the field of ITC and presenting many recent voice contacts made with the next world from both the United States and Europe.

For more information contact
Continuing Life Research
P.O. Box 11036,
Boulder CO 80301, USA,
(303) 673-0660.